And the Angels Called Him...
SHINING BEAR

And the Angels Called Him...
SHINING BEAR

My Inner Journey from Death to Peace

By

Harrison Viers Newberry

© 2023 by Harrison Viers Newberry

All rights reserved. This book or any portion thereof may not be reproduced or used in any manner whatsoever without the express written permission of the publisher except for the use of brief quotations in a book review.

ISBN: 979-8-218-29896-8

This book is dedicated to the people who have
made my life worth living:
Wendy, David, Bob, Carolyn, Cindy, Kenny, Hannah,
Emma, Ada, Season, and Ruby.

I also wish to extend my gratitude to those people whose
help made this book possible:
My wife, Ellen, Carlisle, Eleanor, and Alberto.

Foreword

I've known Harry Newberry for over fifty years. We met in college when we were both in undergraduate school. I was dating Kathy's (Harry's first wife) older brother, which started our bonding. And we've maintained and valued our friendship all these years.

When Harry asked me to write the foreword for this book, I didn't hesitate to say yes. To be part of his story, to have even lived some of it with him, validated my decision.

As difficult as it was for Harry to relive the many hells he's survived, this is his message: Only *you* control *your* happiness and fulfillment, and *you* do that with what you *think*, what you *say*, and the *company you keep!* Everything you go through, both good and bad, is in your life to make you a victor, not a victim.

So quit blaming others for where you are in life, snatch yourself up by the bootstraps, and take responsibility for yourself. Harry tells you exactly how to do it—will it be easy? No. Will you suffer through some "stuff"? Yes. Is it worth all of it? Absolutely!

And please don't think this book is only for recovering alcoholics/addicts. It's for *all* of us because it shows everyone how to live with victory.

Harry wants you to be the person God created you to be, to grow from the inside out, but he especially wants you to have the incredible, peaceful life you deserve.

—Ellen Prescott

Foreword

I am not a celebrity, not a famous person, not even an infamous person. So why am I writing the foreword for this book entitled *Shining Bear?*

Because he asked. Because I can. Because I wanted to.

Harry Newberry and I have been friends for forty-five years or more. We met in the mid to late seventies when he went to work for my father, a pharmaceutical company manager, after a very important interview. I am certain it was quite the "grill." As was always the case in those interviews, Harry brought his lovely wife, Kathy, into our home when he interviewed; it was mandatory. When Harry and Kathy made their move to Durham, North Carolina, they immediately became an extended part of the Holeman family. As for me, I lived in Charlotte at the time, having just begun my teaching career, ultimately relocating to several other cities and one country over the next decades, so Harry's and my life paths splayed in different directions. We seldom saw each other, but we never lost touch. In fact, we met in the Red Rocks one day when I visited Arizona, just prior to a strenuous hike in the Red Rocks.

My dad and Harry had a special relationship, one of love, respect, and empowerment. Even after Harry left the company, they were a constant with each other. Dad was a mentor and a father figure for Harry, and Harry was the son my father needed to pass on his life's wisdom and industry expertise. My only brother was a victim of cerebral palsy and developmental disability, so he was unable to accept these gifts. Harry was the lucky one, and he became more grateful as time marched on.

Decades later when I cared for my father before his passing in 2016, I witnessed Harry and Dad conversing regularly on the telephone. Distance prevented them from seeing each other, as they would have liked, but there were always words of encouragement shared and industry news shared between those men. As this relationship was nearing an end due to my father's illness, Harry's and my relationship was rekindled.

This memoir needed to be written. Yes, it is a journey, but it is far more than that. Harry's life story encompasses the rawness of life—tragedy, loss, loneliness, depression, fear, suffering, defeat, and loss of self-respect and spirituality. But here is the good part. This story also encompasses the path back from that rawness. Harry shares his story from losing his parents, his brother, and his wife; becoming an alcoholic; and losing his jobs, his friends, and himself. He even makes a physical journey to the country of Peru for a spiritual cleansing to renew his life, recognizing he was spiritually dead and knowing he had to do something radical to make a difference.

There are many "scenes" in this book that are graphic, and they are there for a reason. Harry's hope and prayer is that his memoir will affect and effect more than one person to make a similar journey to change their life. He knows strongly that no one has to remain in an unhappy state their entire life. And they do not need to wait until they want to see the end of the world to make that change. Harry rebuilt Harry from the "inside out" as he called it. Earlier on, he had built Harry from the "outside in."

So I urge you to buckle up and read Harry Newberry's book. He is not a nobody. He is a somebody. And he wants to spread his wisdom and experience of a happiness and peace beyond understanding.

—Carlisle Holeman

Table of Contents

Prologue		xv
Chapter 1:	Introduction	1
Chapter 2:	Childhood	3
Chapter 3:	College and Early Adulthood	13
Chapter 4:	The Tragedy Begins	23
Chapter 5:	Emptiness	39
Chapter 6:	Worst Mistake of My Life	43
Chapter 7:	Asking for Help	53
Chapter 8:	Rebuilding My Life	79
Chapter 9:	AA	99
Chapter 10:	New Career and New Marriage	107
Chapter 11:	A New Way of Seeing	125
Chapter 12:	Mind Control	129
Chapter 13:	The Search for Truth and Answers	133
Chapter 14:	Peru Journey	143
Chapter 15:	The Shamanic Path Begins	153
Chapter 16:	Meeting the Q'ero	171
Chapter 17:	First Trip into the Amazon	175
Chapter 18:	Risk versus Reward	179

Chapter 19:	My Journey into the Spirit World	183
Chapter 20:	Processing My Journey	195
Chapter 21:	Another Trauma	201
Chapter 22:	Realizations	209
Chapter 23:	Conclusion	221

Epilogue	229

Prologue

I would like to ask you a simple question. Before you answer, I ask you to stop and really think about it. What do you want out of your life? I was asked this same question close to forty years ago. It was at a point in my life when I was essentially dead. I was completely hopeless and had nothing and no one in my life. I thought about the question for several minutes, in complete silence. I finally answered and said, "I just want to be happy." Is this not what you want? Is this not what everyone wants?

Another thing we all want is to love and be loved. Today I am so happy and am surrounded by love. I have been for several decades. At the time I was asked that question, I had lost everyone and everything that had ever mattered to me. I could not see a way forward. Nothing mattered to me. For the first time in my life, I was all alone, just me and my best friend, Jack Daniels. I went completely off the deep end into alcoholism. This led to many bad decisions in a short period of time. I lost everything I had: my home, my cars, my career, and my self-respect. No one who knew me then—my family or friends—would have given a nickel for my life. My life was over. I spent most of my time contemplating suicide. In this time, I heard these lyrics to a song made famous by the late Janis Joplin: "Another word for freedom is nothing left to lose." This is the story of how I used that freedom to rebuild my life. Before I had built my life from the outside in. However, this time my life was reconstructed from the inside out.

This book contains all the tools, practices, and principles I was given to accomplish this. Not only was my life rebuilt, but I also had discovered a happiness and peace I had never thought possible. When I reflect on the life I had leading up to my world ending, I was asleep, deaf, blind, and dumb insofar as my spiritual genome. Spiritual gurus and spiritual teachers have been saying for thousands of years that we must first die to live. This was certainly proven true in my case.

Chapter 1

Introduction

This is the story of how I went from complete hopelessness—every aspect of my life in complete devastation—to a life of happiness and serenity. When I was in this state of being—hopelessness—my soul was dead. It is the worst feeling you can imagine. What I did not know then was it also offered me an opportunity to be reborn, to live again. Spiritual gurus have been saying for centuries that one must first die to live again. The way I had arrived in this state was not all my fault, but some of it was.

When in my early thirties, I lost both my mom and dad eight months apart. I was devastated, and before I got through that trauma, my wife was diagnosed with cancer. We had fought it and initially thought she would live. A year later the cancer returned in a very aggressive way. Her doctors threw everything they had at her to save her. We knew that if this failed to work, she was to be considered terminal. It did not work. We knew that, barring a miracle, she would die. A week after we received that horrifying news, my only brother died of a massive heart attack.

Looking back, I know I went into shock. The next six months were the worst of my life. My wife, Kathy, suffered beyond belief. She died in my arms, in our home, six months after my brother. To add insult to injury, my drinking had escalated tremendously leading up to her death. Just weeks after the funeral, I crossed what many of us call *the invisible line* into full-blown alcoholism. Even worse was the fact I was all alone. I had no family or any true friends living near me. This is a formula for total disaster. It was!

Chapter 2

Childhood

When I was growing up, it never occurred to me that any of these things would happen to me. I had a very happy childhood. I was the youngest of three kids. I do not know what kind of birth control my parents used. My brother was eighteen years old when I was born, and my sister was almost eight years old. I grew up like an only child in the mountains of Virginia. My dad was in the coal-mining business with my uncle, and we had a farm. I have vivid memories of being an infant, even being born. I remember being in the crib, breaking my last bottle, and my mom carrying me two miles over a mountain to church. People think they can say anything in the presence of a baby because they cannot understand. Do not believe it. Before I could talk, I did understand most everything being said. My mom had a meltdown when she caught me climbing out of my crib. They had to build a lift for it and place a latch out of my reach. When I later recalled and described all these things to everyone, they just could not believe it. I was a very happy child, always had a smile on my face. I worshiped my sister, but she was no good to play with. We did not have next-door neighbors, so I spent a lot of time alone. I learned how to entertain myself. I developed a vivid imagination. There was never a minute that I did not know that I was loved, safe, and protected.

When I was old enough for school, I did well. My teachers told my parents I had a very high IQ, but my attention span was short. I was never a mean kid but was mischievous. My mom and dad were not educated people but placed a high value on education. Growing up on a farm meant hard work daily. Looking back, I suppose we did not have a lot of money, but we had each other. No child ever loved his parents and family more than did I.

My brother got married young, and I was an uncle before I was four years old. My nephew, Marty Joel, was more like my younger brother than a nephew. My brother was more like a second father until I went to college. I had values, morals, and ethics drilled into me. I knew that breaking a rule meant punishment. I was always held accountable for everything I did. If I got a paddling at school, my parents always found out. What I received at home was worse. The great rules I broke back then were things like running in the hall, talking in class, or throwing spit wads. Any form of bad behavior just was not tolerated. Still my teachers liked me. I had started school, first grade, in a two-room schoolhouse. Sometime that year we were moved into a larger school. I had the same teacher in the first, third, and fourth grades, Mrs. Anderson. I loved her, and she was like a second mom, looking after me. When I was an infant, I had asthma but outgrew it. Many years later, she found out where I was living via a relative. She wrote me a letter. I was in my fifties when I received it. She asked if I had gotten past the asthma and recalled how she had to force me to wear a coat when going outside. She recalled how I was not afraid of anything. I was so touched. When I finished the fourth grade, my sister graduated high school. I remember missing her so much. This is the point when my life would change, and I learned about fear.

My mom began having health problems. She was especially having trouble breathing. She would become very ill, and we would have to drive her to the hospital. Because we only had two-lane roads, and it was in the mountains, it was close to an hour drive. I have clear memories of being in the back seat, my mom in the front passenger seat with her head out the window. She would be gasping for a breath. Although we were driving as fast as we could, we were so scared we would not get her there in time. This began when I was nine and continued for four years, getting progressively worse. Finally her doctor said her only hope was to move to a dry climate. We knew she would not get through another winter.

This was very traumatic for me, as it would have been on any ten- or twelve-year-old boy. I had a first cousin living in Albuquerque, New Mexico. My dad took her there. My cousin's wife, Pat, was a registered nurse. She began asking my mom about her symptoms. Pat said this did not sound like asthma at all. She convinced her to go to the Lovelace Clinic and see a pulmonary doctor. Daddy took her to the appointment, and she was examined. Within five minutes the doctor told her, "You do not have asthma. There is something in your throat, blocking your airway. We must get it out immediately." The next day she had surgery, and a large tumor was removed. The doctor told my dad that another week would have been a long life for her. She would need to remain there for many months. She would have to wear a trach tube for the rest of her life. This meant she had to learn to talk again. She would have to receive radiation treatments over a long period of time.

I had never been away from my parents ever. I was staying with my aunt and uncle, who lived close by. I was taking care of the farm, feeding all the animals. My dad had a business to run and came back, leaving my mom there with my cousin. When he returned I was so happy to see him. I clung to him like never before. A couple of weeks later, my cousin called and told my dad that Mommy was not doing well at all. She was depressed, very lonely, and not doing the exercises to learn to talk again. When my dad told me he had to return to Albuquerque, I was devastated. My aunt, his sister, and my uncle came over the next day. He shared the story and explained how concerned he was to leave me. They convinced him to take me along, that I could go to school out there. I was over the moon. By the time we arrived, my mom was not only talking but had improved in a significant way. When I saw her, I fell to my knees beside her. We were so happy to see each other.

I started school there and did finally settle in. It was not easy for me. I was from a small town. Most of my classmates I had known from the first grade. Suddenly I was cast into an environment where I knew no one, was a total stranger. It was a totally different world. I remember sitting in class seeing snow on top of the mountain with people snow skiing. At the same time, people were water skiing on the river. I was both fascinated and fearful. It was a great experience for me in so many ways. Some of the kids were already in gangs, carrying knives. I was approached about joining and promptly declined. I experienced a completely different world. It changed my reality and my view of the world. This coupled with the fact I had entered puberty produced a lot of fear in my life. Eventually my mom had completed all her treatments, and we would leave for home. I did not know until years later that the doctors had given her five years to live. We left Albuquerque on the morning of November 22, 1963. We stopped around midday, and I heard the president had been shot. We were in the panhandle of Texas. Although my parents had not voted for Kennedy, we were just as shocked and hurt as everyone else. The hate that exists today was just not prevalent back then. Someone had killed our president. The assassination took place on Friday, and we arrived home on Sunday.

We were very happy to be home, and the entire family was there waiting for us. We gradually returned to normalcy. I went back to school, and life continued. In 1964, the British invasion began. The Beatles were on the *Ed Sullivan Show*. I had played trombone in the school band for years. I loved music and was impacted by rock bands in a big way. I was one of the first kids in my school to have a Beatles haircut. In my school picture a couple of years later, I looked like a dead ringer for Paul McCartney. Although I loved music, I gave up playing trombone for football. Sports had always been a big part of my life and kept me away from the party scene. I played football and ran track throughout high school. I had never seen marijuana until after I graduated.

During the summers between my sophomore and junior years and my junior and senior years, I was placed in a college prep program at the University of Virginia. During my second summer there, I became friends with a fellow who had just finished his freshman year. One Saturday night, we decided to get some beer. We bought a six-pack each of Colt 45 malt liquor, tall boys. I had tasted alcohol before and never cared for it. My parents were Southern Baptist, and alcohol was strictly prohibited. We drank the beer. I drank six and threw up a case. The school found out, and I got into a lot of trouble. Yet I finished the program and returned to school. I had no desire to ever drink again. It was hard enough to get through summer football camp anyway.

Camp began two weeks before school started. In the hot August heat, it was pure punishment. The very idea of drinking or smoking seemed outrageous. However, after football season was over, the door to the party scene opened. I did have a few Saturday nights of drinking. We would go to a bootlegger and buy a pint each. I got sick every time and suffered horrible hangovers. I did run track again that year, which kept me away from most of it. I suppose I was considered a popular kid and dated the prettiest girls. High school brings pleasant memories. Like most teenagers, I was trying to find who I was. It was all about appearances. I loved clothes and dressed in the latest styles, thinking this elevated me. I graduated before my eighteenth birthday at age seventeen.

I had been accepted to the university, which would begin in September. My dad gave me a job working in his coal mine. My mom had a conniption. I agreed to do it because it would pay double what I could earn elsewhere. I would live at home, which meant I could save what I earned. My friends all said, "Big deal—your dad owns the mine." They did not know my dad because I was given the worst job there. The day began at 4:00 a.m., and we had a long drive. Still it was dark when we entered the mine. I am six-foot-three, and the coal seam was around forty-eight inches. So I could not stand up and walk around. I spent most of the day on my knees. When they blasted the coal, a six- to eight-inch seam of rock would fall on top of the coal. My job was to beat the rock into smaller pieces with a sixteen-pound sledgehammer. It was the hardest job you can imagine. I was so sore after my first two days that I could barely get out of bed. The men were all teasing me, and I know for a fact that not one of them expected me to return. The exception was my dad. He knew me so well and played me perfectly. Before this I could not imagine anything more difficult than football camp. I really did want to quit but would have rather died than give those men the satisfaction.

I stuck with it, and it got easier. It was also dangerous. Sometimes when they blasted the coal, that thick seam of rock did not come down. This meant I had to drive wedges in the crack, on my knees, swinging the sledgehammer. Once I got it open enough, I would use a large crowbar to pull it down. One day I was doing this, and it was much looser than I thought. Suddenly the rock began to fall, and I began falling forward. Fortunately one of the men saw what was about to happen and pulled me back. Had he not been there, I would have been flat on my stomach and at least a thousand pounds of rock would have flattened me. It scared me to death. My dad had two reasons for having me work there. First he said he wanted to teach me the value of a dollar. Secondly, his biggest motivation was that he wanted me to see the life I could look forward to if I failed to finish college. I had always known I would go to college, but I was to be the first one in my family to get a degree.

Chapter 3

College and Early Adulthood

I BEGAN COLLEGE in September. My guidance counselors in high school wanted me first to go to a junior college. Coming from a small town and attending relatively small classes and suddenly being thrust into a large university could be overwhelming. It was difficult in the beginning. As a freshman many of my classes were in auditoriums with maybe a couple hundred students. I had a roommate my first year from home. Scotty was two years older than me and had graduated from a junior college. He was a big help to me. There were three of us who went there from my senior class, and I was the only one to graduate. The guidance counselors had a point. My first year was uneventful. I adjusted and found my footing. I just had no idea who I was and strived for acceptance and to fit in. My mom was having health problems, and I went home often. I lived in constant fear of losing her. I did not realize it then, nor could I admit it, but fear permeated my life.

In 1969, Pete Townsend of the rock band The Who wrote a rock opera called *Tommy*. It was about a young boy who had been traumatized badly. He was completely shut down emotionally. He was going through life deaf, blind, and dumb. He suffered sexual molestation and bullying. Eventually the spell was broken, and he was free. These were topics few people discussed back then, certainly not in rock and roll. Pete was writing about his own life and personal problems. I knew I had been traumatized but did not think I was shut down in any way. I now know that I was completely shut down spiritually. It would be years before my spell was broken. I had not been drinking very much during my first year—a few beers here and there. Then I pledged a fraternity, a wild one. This was like a boot camp for alcoholics. Indeed two of my closest brothers would later die from alcoholism. My life became one big party. We were drinking almost every night. My grades suffered so that when it came to be my time to go active, to become a full brother, I could not due to my grades. I had to go to summer school to get my grades back up. I did become a full brother and lived the next year in the fraternity house. By my senior year, I was basically running the fraternity. Someone had to stay sober. So I smoked pot, which kept me away from alcohol.

This was when I met Kathy. It was love at first sight. From the first night, we were almost never apart again. When I graduated she remained in school. I was with her every weekend. Three years after we met, we were married. We moved to North Carolina and started a life together.

I knew I wanted to continue my education. However, I quickly decided I did not want to remain in the field I had received my undergraduate degree in. I had met a man who owned a pharmacy, and he opened my eyes to the medical arena. I eventually got a degree in pharmacy but decided to go to work for a major drug company. The man who hired me was Dick Holeman. He became my mentor, like a second father. This relationship lasted for many years until he died in his nineties. His daughter, Carlisle, and I are very close friends to this day. My first day on the job was in New York City. I received great training in New York, but Dick Holeman taught me the real world when I returned. I did very well and won every award they had. Then I was approached by Dick's superiors about moving in-house to New York permanently. I loved New York City, and it had broadened my horizons considerably. I had spent a lot of time there but knew I did not want to live there. I was with a small division of a major company, and they were very tight with money. I had heard a major company—one considered the Cadillac of the drug companies—had an opening.

I decided to interview for it. My first interview lasted six hours. They went back and talked with my high school teachers and football coaches. I was amazed when they made me an offer. Back then these positions were very hard to get. They were headquartered in the New York City area but across the Hudson in North Jersey. Had I moved there with the other company, I would have had to live in Jersey anyway. Everything was first-class. My first trip there for training, I flew into La Guardia. They picked me up in a stretch limo. At that time, you only saw stretch limos with very important people. I was impressed. The training lasted two years. I made many trips there. I had more training there than I did in six years of college. I would go there for two weeks of training then go home and employ what I had learned with the doctors in my area. They later boasted that they had spent $200,000 training me. Most of the training was on technology, but then I was selected as one of ten in the US to go through what amounted to a polishing school. They hired two consultants out of New York City for $1,000 an hour. It is important to note that this all occurred at a time when you could get a college degree for $20,000, give or take. We were taught effective speaking in every scenario and how to utilize our natural gifts. They took us into the city at night to five-star restaurants and taught us how to conduct ourselves.

This was huge for me, having grown up in the coal-mining country of Appalachia. I felt like I was on top of the world. When Kathy and I were married, we had nothing. She had majored in psychology, which is worthless without a master's degree. I was working for the government, and we just could not make ends meet on my salary. I ended up working two jobs and going to school at the same time. My mom and dad came down to visit us a month after our wedding. Two weeks later my mom suffered a massive stroke. She never spoke another word and was paralyzed on one side. My dad cared for her for the next four years. Kathy and I had gone for a visit at Christmas. Daddy was not feeling well and looked bad. I was concerned. In February, I received a call he was in the hospital. I immediately drove there, and he had just come out of surgery. It was cancer. The surgeon told me his intention was to remove it, but he was just eaten up inside. I had gone home to handle some business affairs. Two weeks later the hospital called me and said I needed to come now. It was about a five-hour drive, and I was there five hours after receiving the call. He was in ICU. I immediately went there, and as I walked in and stood by him, he flatlined. To this day, I believe he was waiting on me. I collapsed but knew I had to regain my composure as there were things to do. My brother was two hours away, and my sister had two young children to care for. My mom was staying with my aunt at the time, so after making arrangements for my dad, I drove there. I already knew she did not know when I walked in. Although she could not talk, she always knew me and understood what I was saying. Telling her that Daddy had died was the most difficult thing I had ever done. We cried together, and by the next day, she had another stroke. We could not take her to the funeral.

The worst part of this was figuring out what to do with my mom. My aunt was in no condition to care for her. My sister worked a full-time job and had her kids to care for. We all decided the only real option was to place her in a nursing home. To this day, I feel guilty about it. I felt I had abandoned her. My brother and I just could not bear to think of taking care of our mom because of the nature of what was necessary. It involved a very personal and feminine process. We visited her often, especially my sister, who lived close by. I drove up every chance I got. Every time I went, regardless of where she was seated, she would spot me and begin waving her hand and patting her chest. She was so happy to see me. However, each time I left, it tore my heart out. I would cry most of the way home, drinking brandy.

Eight months later I was out of town for work. I was in a doctor's office having a conversation when I looked up and saw my boss and another friend. I knew something was wrong. They took me outside and informed me my mom had died that morning. Inside of eight months, I had lost both my parents. I just did not know how to deal with it emotionally. My drinking escalated. My parents were not just Southern Baptist but old Regular Baptist. Their interpretation of the Bible was literal, no spiritual key. So out of respect for them, we had a preacher do her funeral. Not only did he offer no spiritual comfort but got on a rail about the sin of women with painted faces. My sister, sister-in-law, and wife wore very light makeup—just a little powder and light lipstick. Everyone in the packed church knew exactly who he was talking about. I was enraged. I am not a violent person but still regret not taking him outside and slapping him to his knees. This left a powerful bad taste in my mouth about religion.

Over the next couple years, we had to decide what to do with our family home. The land had been in our family for generations. My sister and I were both born in the house. A doctor was present, but this was our home in every sense of the word. To say it was a hard decision was an understatement. But when it was broken into, we finally had to sell it. This was like going through another death. I still miss it but have it always in my heart. I can go there in my mind and see every detail.

At least I had my Kathy to go home to. I poured myself into building my career. We finally had our first home built. It was not a big home but was custom built in a restricted development. It was on a beautiful one-acre wooded lot. Gradually we decorated every room, and Kathy did it first-class. I loved doing the landscaping and taking care of the property. We were so happy. In time, I got bored with my work. I was thinking of going to medical school and had several doctor friends pushing me to do so. Kathy and I talked about this and figured out how we might be able to handle it. I took the MCAT, the medical school entrance exam. Around this time, I had received a call about a position with a high-tech orthopedic surgical device company. I turned them down twice because it meant relocation. A year later I received another call informing me there was now an opening in North Carolina. The man who had the area had been promoted.

The VP of sales flew in to meet with me. They already knew a lot about me, so I was made an offer on the spot. I was scared to death. This was the major leagues, the big time. However, there was risk, and I knew they demanded performance. The CEO was on the front cover of *Money* magazine with the caption under his picture that said, "20 percent or else." I felt guilty about leaving. My company had invested so much in me, and I had spent years getting my education in the field. It had taken Kathy and I eight years to pay off my college expenses, but we did, where many did not. The upside was huge financial reward. Kathy supported me completely in whatever decision I made. I finally decided to go for it. No one ever knows how a person will fit into a new role until you put them to work. Well, it clicked for me from the beginning.

Everything I touched turned to gold. I could not believe it. I was competing with the best of the best and winning. I had been earning a good income before and had a company car and great benefits. I more than doubled my income my first year. Then I received a bonus check that was more than what I previously earned in a year. We were flying high. Kathy did not have to work anymore, and we were ready to start a family. I had always wanted children. We invested a lot of money, had no debt, a very high credit rating, and money in the bank—a lot of it. After my second year there, I was still on a roll. I was in surgery almost every day, setting up the equipment and teaching these surgeons how to perform the procedures. It was cutting-edge technology at the time. Very exciting and I loved it. I was number one in the nation in this area.

My boss and I had to attend a meeting with a hospital in Charlotte, so I had been away for a few days. He was with me when I pulled down my driveway, where he had left his car. Kathy came running out in tears. I asked what was going on, and she informed me she had to go into surgery. She had found a large lump in her breast. She was terrified, but mostly of the surgery itself. She had never been in an operating room, so I explained everything to her. She trusted me completely as I did her. Her gynecologist was a good friend. He had told me that, at her age, there was probably nothing to worry about. She was only twenty-nine at the time. I just could not imagine it could be malignant. I was not over the death of my parents. I had poured myself into my work, day and night. The hard work and alcohol had prevented me from going through the pain of grief. I wanted Kathy to be proud of me. I had always wanted my family and hers to be proud of me. Truthfully I had never felt I was good enough, felt less than. Even with all the success and money, I still felt that way.

Chapter 4

The Tragedy Begins

Two days later, on a Friday, she went into surgery. Her mom and dad came down. Because I knew the operating room (OR) staff, I was allowed to put on scrubs and go back to the OR suite with her. Then we all waited in the OR waiting room. They were only to remove the lump for biopsy. I knew the procedure would not take more than an hour. When two hours passed, I was climbing the walls. Finally the surgeon walked out, and I could see from the look on his face it was not good news. He came to me and said, "We did remove the lump, which was huge, and it was malignant." I felt the blood drain from my face. I thought I was going to faint but somehow held myself together. Then her mom and dad came over to me, and I had to tell them. It hit them hard, and we just hugged and held each other. Kathy was the youngest of four children and their only daughter. They were like parents to me, and I truly loved them. The surgeon came back and told us he had her on the schedule for a modified radical mastectomy the following Tuesday. For some reason this upset me more. I did not want to lose it in front of her parents, so I excused myself. I went outside and sat in my car and proceeded to have a meltdown. I still remember that moment vividly. I just could not believe it. I finally pulled myself back together and returned to the waiting room. When she got out of recovery and into a room, we were able to be with her. I never left her side. I only went home to shower and change clothes.

The thing I remember most is that Kathy handled it much better than I did. There was a light around her, a peace, that everyone noticed, even her doctors and nurses. After the surgery that following Tuesday, the peace not only remained but grew stronger. The nurses kept asking her, "Kathy, are you sure you do not need pain meds?" She declined, and this is extremely rare. I have visited many hospital rooms but have never experienced the peace I did in her room. Everyone commented about it. A couple days later, her surgeon came in and told her he wanted her to get out of bed, go down the hall to this large bathroom, remove the bandages, and bathe. This would be the first time she would see herself without her breast. She was a thirty-eight D-cup. The entire family was there, her brothers and sisters-in-law. A few minutes later, her mom said, "Come on, Kathy, let's get you up and do this." Kathy immediately spoke up and said, "No, I want Harry!" They always knew how much we loved each other, but in that moment, they understood how deeply. So I got her down to

And the Angels Called Him...Shining Bear

Kathy Cooper Newberry 1975

the bathroom, and we slowly removed the bandages. It was not a pretty sight. We just looked at each other, not saying a word. I held her tightly in my arms. We saw it for the first time together. We faced everything together, just as we had always done. At this time we had every reason to believe she would be ok. The surgeon felt he got all the cancer, so at that time, protocol called for no chemotherapy or radiation.

A few days later she was discharged. We went home and returned to our normal routines. I went back to work. Several months later I took her to the Bowman Gray Center for Medical Education at Wake Forest University for breast reconstructive surgery. At that time, we elected to have them do a subcutaneous mastectomy on the other side. We wanted to be proactive and take no chance that the cancer might return in the other breast. This time she was in a lot of pain, but I never left her side. We returned home feeling confident she would be fine. We even went to her oncologist and asked if she could get pregnant. She gave us the go and said it might be a benefit in preventing the cancer from reoccurring. We really wanted a family. That Christmas, we went to Virginia to spend the holiday with my brother and his family. Since my parents had passed, we had spent our holidays with her family. This was Kathy's idea. Kathy had grown up in the country club scene, which was 180 degrees from the world I came from. I now know she did it for me. Anyway my brother was over the moon. It was the best Christmas of my life. At the time, I had no way of knowing the significance of that holiday.

Several weeks later I noticed Kathy was not feeling well. She asked me to make an appointment for her with our family doctor. Although it did not appear to be anything serious, I had a bad feeling. I made the appointment with her oncologist, Dr. Selman. I did not tell her until we were driving to the appointment. She got angry at me, stating she had no reason to visit him. Her anger was a sign that she, too, was concerned. I just told her we needed to make sure. When we arrived, she and I went into the exam room and waited. He came in and examined her and then left the room for a couple minutes. When he returned, he looked directly at Kathy and said, "Well, I am worried about you."

The bottom just fell out of our world. By this time, we knew a lot of statistics on breast cancer. We knew that following the original diagnosis she had an 80 percent chance of survival. However, if the cancer reoccurred, the odds dropped to around 25 percent. This is now where we were. So they began to treat her very aggressively with chemotherapy and radiation. We knew that if this failed to put her into remission, the odds dropped to 5 percent or less. Basically barring a miracle, she would die. The treatment almost killed her. We even questioned whether it was worth it. It was just horrible. A couple of weeks passed, and she was reexamined. The treatment had failed. The cancer continued to metastasize. Although this was many years ago, I still remember that day like it was yesterday. We left his office and got into our car. There are no words to describe how we felt. Kathy looked at me with tears in her eyes and said, "Oh my God, Harry, what are we going to do?" I could not say a word. We were both in shock.

A week later, we were still walking around the house in a daze. Then early one morning I received a phone call from Marty, my brother's son. I knew immediately something was wrong. He said it was about his dad. He had suffered a massive heart attack. I asked how he was. Marty said he wasn't; he was dead. I was so stunned; I cannot describe how I felt. I was already in a state of shock, but this news took it to another level. Kathy and I drove to Virginia immediately. I made the funeral arrangements. We attended his funeral of course, but I cannot remember any of it. I think all my self-protection mechanisms took over. I was just numb, in a blackout. I stayed for a few days to help my sister-in-law get his affairs in order. When our parents had died, Norman, my brother, was there for my sister and me to lean on. He was our pillar of strength. Now they were all gone, and I had to drive home and try to face what would come. I had been a heavy drinker since college, but my drinking accelerated to another level. I just could not bear the pain. I simply had no way to carry this. I turned to the only thing that would ease my pain and provide the courage I needed.

The next six months was like my worst nightmare come true. I watched Kathy deteriorate daily. She had been a beautiful young woman and now looked like she was eighty. Her hair fell out, and she was bloated. However, the worst part was watching her suffer. Her mom was there most of the time. Occasionally I would go out of town on business. When I returned it appeared she had aged several years. I lived on the phone searching for new drugs and treatments. Eventually I got her into a clinical trial on a drug I had heard about several years earlier. It had been in research at the time. When the treatments began, we were happy the side effects were relatively nonexistent. However, the treatments failed. I knew it might be a long shot, but I had to try. I needed to know I had done everything in my power to save her life, and I did. As the pain worsened, I was administering the narcotics. Her doctors had told me that what might finally take her was an overdose of narcotics. We knew she was running out of time rapidly. I remember many terrible days but recall one morning vividly. I had given her a high dose of pain meds. A week prior, just half that dose would have kept her pain level down for five to six hours. I was worried but could not let her suffer. An hour later she was literally screaming, "Harry, please come. It hurts so bad I cannot stand it." Her mom and I were standing in the kitchen. Not a word was spoken because we knew another dose might kill her. Finally her mom looked at me and asked, "Harry, do you want me to do it?" I said, "No, I will take care of it." I went into our bedroom and gave her another dose. A few minutes later, she settled down and fell sleep. She was breathing normally so I went back into the kitchen. The tension in that house I cannot begin to explain. I had been drinking a glass of orange juice when this all began. Her mom pointed to it and suggested

I finish it. I glanced over to a bottle of vodka sitting in the corner. It had been left out of the bar from the weekend before. So I filled the remainder of the glass of OJ with vodka. After drinking it I felt the tension just melt away. I had never drunk in the mornings. I now know this was a major crossroads for me. I crossed what we in Alcoholics Anonymous (AA) call the invisible line. The point of no return.

Kathy had remained lucid throughout this period. Before the pain got out of control, we would lie in bed at night and talk. She knew she was dying and, frankly, was handling it much better than I was. She had majored in psychology and was looking at all this in an analytical manner. She seemed to know the death of her body was not the end. She would ask me, "What do you think it will be like?" I could not answer that, but even then, I somehow knew I would see her again. She told me this, "If there is a way, I will contact you." This would eventually become very significant. She would contact me many times. She also planned her funeral. First she informed me she wanted to be cremated. I had never known anyone who had been cremated and neither had her parents. We fought her on this, but she remained steadfast. She wanted me to take her ashes to the beach in front of the family beach house and scatter them over the ocean. This would mean there would be no gravestone. She finally agreed to allow half of her ashes to be buried in a cemetery near the home of her parents. I would take the other half to the beach. She was truly a remarkable young woman. I was so lucky to have her as my wife. She also chose the priest who would perform the funeral service. It would be at our church, an Episcopal church we had been active in. She wanted a poem by Max Ehrmann called "Desiderata" read. She had a plaque of it, which I still have to this day. There would be two funeral services, one in Greensboro, where we lived, and the other in Johnson City, Tennessee, where she grew up. She planned everything.

Two weeks following the incident with the painkillers, we had gone to bed one evening. Her mom and I were taking turns watching her. There were double French doors off our bedroom leading into a sunroom full of plants and wicker furniture. I had fallen asleep in a chaise lounge just outside the open doors. Suddenly I was awakened by her mom screaming at me to come fast. Kathy was trying to get out of bed. I arrived just in time to catch her. We both fell onto the carpet. I was holding her in my arms when she stopped breathing. I tried to administer CPR, but it was too late. I just laid there with her, begging her not to go. Her mom called an ambulance. When they arrived I was still holding her. They had to pull me away. I rode in the ambulance with her to the hospital where she was pronounced dead on arrival. We all had known this was coming, and I had tried to prepare myself. However, there is just no way one can prepare themselves for this kind of reality. At the time I mostly held myself together. I told myself all the obvious things. At least she was no longer suffering and was now

DESIDERATA

GO PLACIDLY AMID THE NOISE & HASTE, & REMEMBER WHAT PEACE THERE MAY BE IN SILENCE. AS FAR AS POSSIBLE WITHOUT surrender be on good terms with all persons. Speak your truth quietly & clearly; and listen to others, even the dull & ignorant; they too have their story. Avoid loud & aggressive persons, they are vexations to the spirit. If you compare yourself with others, you may become vain & bitter; for always there will be greater & lesser persons than yourself. Enjoy your achievements as well as your plans. Keep interested in your own career, however humble; it is a real possession in the changing fortunes of time. Exercise caution in your business affairs; for the world is full of trickery. But let this not blind you to what virtue there is; many persons strive for high ideals; and everywhere life is full of heroism. Be yourself. Especially, do not feign affection. Neither be cynical about love; for in the face of all aridity & disenchantment it is perennial as the grass. Take kindly the counsel of the years, gracefully surrendering the things of youth. Nurture strength of spirit to shield you in sudden misfortune. But do not distress yourself with imaginings. Many fears are born of fatigue & loneliness. Beyond a wholesome discipline, be gentle with yourself. You are a child of the universe, no less than the trees & the stars; you have a right to be here. And whether or not it is clear to you, no doubt the universe is unfolding as it should. Therefore be at peace with God, whatever you conceive Him to be, and whatever your labors & aspirations, in the noisy confusion of life keep peace with your soul. With all its sham, drudgery & broken dreams, it is still a beautiful world. Be careful. Strive to be happy.

© 1927 by Max Ehrman all rights reserved. - Copyright renewed 1954 by Bertha K. Ehrman
Reprinted by permission Crescendo Publishing Co. Boston

at peace. Watching her suffer had been so bad, I would find myself praying for God to take her. Then I would feel so guilty, that I must be a bad person. Emotions are not always logical. I had no way of knowing these feelings were normal. I was traveling an unknown path. When I returned home, it was around 3:00 a.m. There was no way I could sleep. It felt like the end of the world. I called my sister and awakened her. I woke a lot of people that morning.

Two days later we had a visitation at the funeral home. As always they allowed the immediate family to go in first. I had attended a lot of these and was used to walking in and seeing a casket containing the body of the loved one. This had always been an incredibly painful thing. When I saw the urn containing her ashes, I had tears in my eyes but suddenly began to laugh. Everyone looked at me like I had *lost it*. Kathy and I had argued so much over the cremation, I laughed because I thought, "Darn, she was right again." It felt like she was there saying, "I told you so." She knew that if I had to walk in and see her lifeless body in a casket, I could not handle it. I had to admit it did make it much easier. Today when I think of her, I have a picture in my mind of the beautiful woman she was. I do not have the image of her dead in a casket. For that, I am grateful.

Both funeral services were packed. We both had so many friends. During the first service at our church, Father Gary read "Desiderata," and people wept. He said he had spoken with Kathy before her death, and she wished this as a kind of legacy to her family and friends. The second service in John City was equally powerful. The difference was in those who attended, mainly people in both our families and extended families. It was comforting being surrounded by loved ones. Following the funeral, I spent a few days there with her parents and brothers. They were my family too, and I truly loved them. I had remained sober throughout this time. I knew I had to leave and drive home. Her mom wanted some of them to go with me, feeling I should not be alone. I knew it would be hard walking back in that house but felt I had to face it alone. I drove back the five-hour ride alone. I cried the entire trip. When I drove down the long driveway and parked, I had a difficult time getting out of the car. Walking back into our home was one of the hardest things I had ever done. A flood of emotions came over me and an emptiness unlike anything I had ever felt. I have heard people with strong marriages introduce their spouse as their better half. I finally understood what that meant. Half of me was missing. I had spent a lot of time by myself, but now for the first time in my life, I felt totally alone. I still had my sister, thank God, but she lived in another state. Everyone else I had ever loved was gone. My best friends were scattered all over the country. Kathy and I just had each other. She was my wife and my best friend, my partner, my mate, and my family. We had watched our home go up from an empty lot. Everything in that house brought back a memory. It was tearing my heart out.

Suddenly I realized I had nothing to live for. I did not care about anything, not my career, money—nothing. I thought about suicide day and night but told no one. I began drinking constantly. I did not fall asleep at night. I passed out. I did not awaken in the morning; I came to. Everyone was worried about me. They would ask how I was doing all the time. I would lie and say I was fine. I had just enough of the Bible in me to recall that suicide was a major sin. If I could have been certain I would go to be with Kathy and my family, I would have pulled the trigger. I had my dad's Smith and Wesson .38 special and my grandfather's 12-gauge shotgun. I remember distinctly walking around the house with that .38 in one hand and a bottle of Jack Daniels in the other. A lot of people knew I was drinking heavily, but most would give me a pass. They all knew what I had gone through and would say, "If that happened to me, I would be drinking too." I was falling apart inside. Deep down, I knew what I was doing was wrong. I had always held myself to very high standards. Now I simply could not function. So I tried to conceal everything, but people were catching on. My company had been wonderful. The CEO said to give myself some time.

By this time, I was not drinking to get high. It had become like medicine. I would get up in the morning with my hands shaking so bad I would have to use both hands to hold a drink to my mouth. This was the only thing that would stop the shakes. It was a catch-22 and a miserable existence. I could not show up in surgery shaking, but neither could I show up stinking of alcohol. Looking back now, I really did not know what was happening to me, why I was shaking. I remember thinking it was because of the grief. I was afraid to tell anyone and did not.

I remember women coming to me following Kathy's death. Some said how proud they were of me for not leaving Kathy. I was shocked! Yes, it was difficult to face her suffering, but the thought of running never entered my mind. There was no amount of money or anything else that could have pulled me away from her. I mostly thought, "What kind of men do you associate with?" Other women told me I would have women coming after me, like a prize catch. I did not believe them. Kathy had told me she wanted me to remarry. At the time I said no way. I could not imagine it. She said if I did not, it would be an insult to her and what we had had.

She had died on October 21. It had been the longest two months of my life. It felt like two years. That Christmas I went to spend it with my sister and Kathy's family. They lived a half hour apart. I do not know how, but I managed to stay reasonably sober but was drinking. I did not want anyone to know the truth about my drinking. I thought I put on a good act, but Kathy's mom, Eunice, knew me too well and told me how worried she was about me. I did feel better there among my family and hers. They had all watched Kathy and I grow up together. Yes, they were my in-laws but felt like my own family. On Christmas morning, we began opening gifts. I found myself becoming very emotional. Kathy was not there, and it hit me hard. After all the gifts had been opened, Eunice turned to me and said, "Harry, you have one more gift to open." She and Betty, my sister-in-law, brought it to me. I noticed there was no card on it to indicate who it was from. They said, "It is from Kathy." The tears started rolling down my cheeks. I opened it, and it was a needlepoint. Eunice told me she had just finished it shortly before she died. She had asked that it be given to me at Christmas. It read:

My Husband
A strong arm to lean upon
A tender shoulder to cry upon
A patient ear to sound upon
A firm chest to rest upon
A loving heart to rely upon
All these things I find in you
My only lover and my best friend

It took me to my knees in tears. Everyone there was crying. Oh God, I missed her so much. I just could not see a way forward. We had had our whole lives ahead of us. There was nothing I had dreamed of that did not include her. I had become so successful in my career. We had made so many plans for our future, including a family.

Chapter 5

Emptiness

I drove home the following day and cried the entire way. When I arrived the house felt even emptier than before. I climbed right back into the bottle. I was still contemplating suicide. One evening, I sat on a chair in the kitchen with my grandad's shotgun. I held the butt on the floor, the end of the barrel under my chin and had my finger on the trigger. I squeezed it and just held it there for a few minutes. I began thinking, what if I fail and somehow survive the blast? I also knew this was a one-time chance, that there would be no second chance. No way to correct the mistake. Perhaps what concerned me most was the question of whether I would end up being with Kathy and my family. Anyway, I backed off but somehow pulled the trigger in the process. The gun went off in front of my nose and blew a big hole in the ceiling. I was stone drunk, but it scared the heck out of me. The following day I called a man to come and repair the hole. I did not want anyone to know, but it did get out. My friend and attorney came and took my guns away from me. I was in bad shape and needed help. At the time, I never once considered asking for help. I lived alone and just hid out. I stayed away from everyone, especially people in the medical community.

My brother-in-law, Rick, lived in Raleigh, which was about two hours away. He would often drive over on weekends. He and I had always been close. He had lived with Kathy and me for a year a few years earlier. He went with me to the beach to spread the second half of Kathy's ashes. We had a lot of friends down there, and they owned boats. Ed, one of our friends with a large boat that could handle the ocean, agreed to take us out. When we were in front of the house about a mile offshore, I opened the ashes. Rick and I looked inside. We had expected it to be just powder, but there were bone fragments, some of which were large. This hit both of us hard. It tore me to pieces. We slowly poured her ashes into the water. When we returned to the beach house, I proceeded to get very drunk. This was my pattern. I would wash down all my feelings.

I had tried so hard to conceal how much I was drinking. People began to catch on and voiced their concerns. However, one thing I did not want was pity. I do not know why; I just did not want it. Many people enabled me by explaining away why I was drinking so much. Worse still, I began telling everyone I was over Kathy's death, that I had grieved while she was dying. Now I was ready to get on with my life. Trust me, this was the biggest lie I'd ever told myself. The crazy thing is that many people believed it. I desperately wanted to believe it. I would learn years later that, when I was under the influence of alcohol or any mind-altering substance, I was cut off from my heart. Everything I felt or sensed was an illusion. Nothing was real, especially not love, which is an emotion from the heart, from our inner self. What I had felt was the result of a biochemical reaction in the brain created by the alcohol. Everything tended to be a lie, just an illusion.

The women who told me I would have women coming after me were right, much to my surprise. I received phone calls, cards, and letters. I remember receiving a sympathy card, maybe a month after the funeral. It was from an OR nurse in Charlotte. Under the sentiments she wrote, "If there is ANYTHING I can do please let me know." *Anything* was underlined three times. At the time, nothing could have been further from my mind. However, as time passed, I became so lonely and desperate I was open to most anything that could provide relief. One of Kathy's former coworkers, a woman, suggested I go to dinner with her cousin Jenna. I agreed, and the following Saturday night Jenna showed up at my home. I had already been drinking and so had she. We went to dinner, to my favorite Italian restaurant, and continued drinking. We drove back to my house, driving drunk as usual. We proceeded to get wasted, and she spent the night. Neither of us expected anything to come from it because I had just been promoted. This meant I would have to relocate to Michigan. I was happy about it but was more worried. How could I possibly conceal my drinking while working in a high-visibility role? Then I had to fly to Vegas to attend the Orthopedic Academy meeting. It did not go well for me. They saw the drinking issue. I knew this was not going to work, so I declined the promotion. It would involve extensive travel all over the country and out of it. Had Kathy lived, I would have been all over this. It was what I had worked so long and hard for. I told them I just was not ready, that it was too soon after the deaths. I was already alone, but this would mean being even more alone.

Chapter 6

Worst Mistake of My Life

So I went home and attempted to get on with my life. My drinking was getting worse by the day. I called Jenna and resumed the affair. She began staying at my house every night. Had my drinking reached even half what it now was while Kathy was alive, I shudder to think how she would have reacted. She would have had me committed or left me. Probably both! No way would she have put up with that and rightfully so. She had kept my drinking under control. If we attended an event where I had had too much to drink and embarrassed her and myself, I would be in the doghouse for at least a week. I would feel terrible about it and knew I deserved everything she was dishing out to me.

Now here I was with Jenna. Not only did she say nothing about how much I was drinking, but she was drinking with me, drink for drink. This is incredible because I was drinking morning, noon, and night at this time. We never left the house until we had consumed a pint of vodka each. Her friends were just as bad, and I never included any of my friends in anything.

Soon I discovered she had a young son, Danny. He was ten or eleven years old and a great kid. Her parents were fine people. Her mom had retired as a teacher, and her dad was a head coach. As several weeks passed, I had a cookout one Saturday. Her parents and another couple or two were there. During that time her mom pulled me to the side for a private talk. She told me how happy she was that Jenna and I were together but said she did not approve of what we were doing. She meant living together out of wedlock. She said I could tell her this was none of her business and that we were both over twenty-one. But what about Danny? He was just a little boy, and he woke up every morning asking, "Where is my mom?" She looked directly at me and asked, "Now, Harry, what would you have me tell him?" I felt about two inches tall and completely agreed with her. I did not know why this had never occurred to me. I had never been a parent. She said, "Look, just make her get up and come home at night, regardless of the time. At least she will be there for him in the morning." In retrospect, this should have thrown up a huge red flag. Why had Jenna never mentioned this to me? She was supposed to be a mother. The next night I sat down with her and discussed this. I told her she simply had to stop drinking early so she could drive home. She nodded in agreement, but I could tell it was no big deal to her. When the time came that she needed to stop drinking, she would just laugh at me and pour another drink. At the time, I did not want her to go home, and even though I was drunk, this went against everything inside me. My mom was always there for me, day and night. Deep down, I knew this was wrong, but it was also the first time I had felt any peace.

A few weeks went by, and I knew I had always wanted a family. Marrying Jenna would give me that, plus solve the dilemma of Jenna not being home with Danny. I do now realize this was insane thinking, but I married her. I can tell you to this very day, this constituted the biggest mistake I ever made in my life. If I am ashamed of anything I ever did, this is it. Everyone tried to talk me out of it, but I would not listen.

After we were married, I had friends come over to the house and plead with me to allow them to take me to the courthouse and get the marriage annulled. I would just become angry, a good indication that I knew they were right. We were married in June. I took her on a honeymoon to Lake Tahoe. We first flew into San Francisco and stayed at a very expensive hotel in Sausalito. Then we drove up through the wine country. I was drunk when I married her and had continued drinking nonstop on this trip. The entire trip is a blur. I do remember stopping in Sacramento and spending a night with my best friend at work. He and I had been number one and number two in the company nationally. He and his wife, Beverly, met Kathy in New York City for a vacation together. They loved Kathy. When I showed up at their home with Jenna, they were shocked. We had only been there five minutes when John asked me to step outside. He looked at me and said, "Harry, what are you doing with her?" People like John, who knew me and Kathy, would take one look and know there was something wrong with this picture. Jenna was very attractive and dressed well, but when she opened her mouth, everyone knew. The simple fact was that we had nothing in common. She was not an educated woman, often butchered the English language. Not that I was all that sophisticated, but she had no class. The hard truth was this: all we had in common was drugs, sex, and rock and roll, with alcohol being the drug of choice.

I do not know what Jenna's intentions were in the beginning. I do know what they were soon after the marriage. She saw dollar signs. She began hitting me up for money the first week following the California trip. My intentions were very simple. I just wanted love and companionship—period. Red flags were going up everywhere, but I ignored them.

A few months later in late August or September, I had an experience I will never forget. Every morning when I awakened, I would feel horrible, like I had been hit by a train. My vision was blurred, and I could not focus. My body would be vibrating, especially my hands. The only way to relieve my condition was to have a huge drink. A drink would consist of a half pint of vodka. This was every morning, a miserable existence. However, on this particular morning, I awakened, and it was just getting light outside. First I looked around the bedroom and realized my vision was crystal clear. Then I realized I felt good—no hangover, no shaking, no vibrating. My mind was clear for the first time in ages. I held my hands out, and they were steady as a rock. Then I sensed a light around me, a warmth, and a comforting feeling. I have no idea how long this lasted, ten minutes or an hour and ten minutes. Then, as crazy as this may sound, it hit me that Kathy was gone. Then I became aware that my brother and my parents were gone. I felt this overwhelming sense of loss. Of course I knew in my head they were gone, but this went deep into my soul, into my heart. When my family and wife had died, I now know a wall went up around me, my self-protection defenses. On this morning, the walls were pulled down.

At some point, I glanced over beside me in bed and saw Jenna. I thought, "Oh my God, what have I done?" I was suddenly back in the real world and reality hit me like a tsunami. For the first time, I could see truth and understand what my family and friends had been trying to tell me. I had just had a huge spiritual experience. I could see what a mess I was in but had no idea what to do about it.

I knew I should end it with Jenna, but I did nothing. Had it just been her, I would have, but there were other people involved, especially her son, whom I adored. I honestly think I married him more than Jenna. I cannot tell you how many times I have regretted not walking away then. God was giving me a chance, but I also know he knew I would not accept it. It was the beginning of the end. In retrospect, this was the turning point. Although I continued to drink, I became painfully aware the drinking had to stop. I simply could not function without alcohol and could not function with it. I was wallowing in self-loathing and began hating myself. At this point, I really thought I was now past the deaths. Eventually I would learn just how deluded I was.

I was very surprised that my company had not fired me. My numbers were in the tank. I was so far behind that I did not see a way to catch up. To avoid being fired, I began interviewing for another position. The interview process was intense. They grilled me and looked in every corner of my past. I was trying everything I could think of to stop drinking or at least to slow down. I knew I had a problem, but I knew nothing about alcoholism. I still do not know how I managed to hold myself together to get through this interview process. These men were sharp and at the top of their games. I was hired and fell uphill financially. I had to fly into New York for training. This technology was highly technical. I was sneaking around drinking the whole time. Mostly I was trying to steady my shaking hands. The wheels were going to come off. My boss had heard reports that they were smelling alcohol on me. It was not that I had to operate this equipment, but I did have to teach others and do it during demos. I knew I was in a mess but had no idea what to do about it. I did complete the training and flew home.

I made it through the Christmas holidays, but in January, my boss showed up. He confronted me about my drinking. Looking back, he was either in recovery himself or had someone close who was. He knew all the buttons to push. In the end, he told me he wanted to help because he and others saw greatness in me, but alcohol was destroying me. He then looked me in the eye and said, "How can we help?" I have always regretted not accepting his offer. I was in such denial that I swore to him I would never touch another drop. Yes, this was pure BS, but the crazy thing was that I meant it. What I did not realize was that I had lost the power of choice in drinking. Two men from the home office showed up two weeks later and fired me. Now I was in deep financial trouble. The wheels were falling off everything in my life, and Jenna was like an anchor around my neck. I blamed only myself. Had I been in my boss's shoes, I would have fired me. The entire time I was drinking I maintained my high standards. I just could not live up to them, and this continued to produce self-hatred within me.

Since I had had the spiritual experience, which I never told Jenna, some strange things had begun happening. For example, I had a fantastic stereo system. It was an analog system, so to turn it on, you had to walk to it and turn the knob clockwise. On the other side of the amplifier was another round knob to turn the volume up or down. There was no remote. While I was away and Jenna was there alone, the stereo would suddenly turn on when she was in another room. Then the volume would turn to full blast. It was freaking her out. Initially I was not sure what to make of her story. I knew I could not believe much of what she said. Then it happened when I was there. I just knew it was Kathy, and so did Jenna. I knew Kathy wanted me to marry again, but I knew she would never approve of Jenna.

My drinking had placed me in many dangerous situations. Every day I live now is a gift. I should be six feet under. I was blacking out frequently. Blackouts are the hallmark of alcoholism. I recall a Friday night in New York. I was working for the company in New Jersey. I took a company car, a big station wagon, and drove into the city. Because I had lived there, I knew the safe areas. I was in a place called Maxwell's Plum on First Avenue. I was drinking at the bar when suddenly everything got quiet and people were staring. It was John and Yoko Lennon being taken to a table. I remember being there until around 1:00 a.m. The next thing I remember was waking up in an XXX-rated movie theater. It was around 6:00 a.m., and

I was the only person in there. I got up, freaked out, and walked outside. I immediately recognized where I was. I was on 42nd Street, just west of Broadway and Seventh. At that time, this was one of the most dangerous places in the city. I suddenly remembered the company car. I was scared beyond belief. I walked down to the corner and looked up Eighth Avenue, and there was my car. I was more than relieved. I jumped into the car and headed for the Lincoln Tunnel and back to my hotel in Jersey. That could have destroyed my career and me too. Looking back, I think the only thing that saved me was the fact that I did my drinking in nice places, around nice people. In New York, I hung out at places like Studio 54 and other high-end places.

Chapter 7

Asking for Help

A WEEK OR two following my termination from my recent position, I was arrested for drunk driving. The police took me to jail to be booked. I called my attorney to come get me out. He came and brought his wife, who was a member of AA. They had known me for years. They called a couple other people and did an intervention on me. They convinced me to enter treatment. My back was against the wall, and I knew it. I did not resist. My world had fallen apart, and I just could not see a way forward.

They had already arranged to get me into Fellowship Hall. I had heard about it, and at that time, it was considered one of the foremost treatment centers in the country. I was admitted that day. Initially I was in detox. Within a few days, the shaking had stopped, and my appetite was returning. The program was all based upon the twelve-step recovery method. They had begun interrogating me on day one, when I was in detox. They had me sign a bunch of release agreements. I felt so bad I did not know what I was signing. I had given them the right to contact my family, Kathy's family, and former bosses. Anyone who could give them insight into me and my past. There were around fifty to sixty patients there, and all the counselors were in recovery themselves.

By the end of my first week, they knew me better than I knew myself. It became obvious to all of them that I hated myself. The good news and the bad news were that I blamed myself for everything. I vividly recall a private session with my personal counselor. She said, "Harry, you are *not* a bad person but a sick person who needs help." I did not buy it. To me, this sounded like a cop-out and excuse for improper behavior. It sounded like stories of a man robbing a convenience store and killing the owner in the commission of the crime. Then some slick-talking lawyer getting him off by saying his father beat him, and he had a bad childhood. I just could not buy the disease concept. I would admit to being an alcoholic but had no idea what that meant. I had this concept imprinted on my brain that described what an alcoholic was. A real alcoholic was some bum you see lying on the sidewalk, filthy dirty, a bad person not to be trusted. Drinking from a paper bag. I decided this was who I was. I just did not tell them this.

I gave myself to the program. I did everything asked of me. I read the big book of AA, which is the AA bible. I read the twelve steps and everything I could on the program and its entire history. We were completely sequestered. No phone calls and no visitors. They took us through the first eight steps while there. AA is such a simple program. It had originally been six steps. I now describe it as three steps: trust God, clean house, and help others. There is only one step we must get perfect. This is step one: come to believe that we are powerless over alcohol and that our lives have become unmanageable. The key word here is *powerless*. This was hard for me. I had never believed I was powerless over anything. I know this sounds arrogant. I had told myself that if I set a goal and worked hard, I could succeed. Indeed I had succeeded in many other areas of my life but had failed miserably with drinking. There was no denying that I had tried everything to stop drinking but lost every single time. I told myself and others that I had step one completed. The first three steps are the *surrender steps*. Step two is "come to believe that a power greater than myself could restore me to sanity." Step three is "make a decision to turn my will and my life over to the care of God, as I understand him." I did believe God could, but my question was why would he want to help a worthless person like me? At the time, I thought I had done these three steps. The problem, as I look back, is that this was all in my head. It had to come from our heart. I did the best I could at the time.

The next six steps are the action steps. Step four is "making a searching and fearless moral inventory of myself." This involves writing down your life story, every detail. You must include every detail, how it made you feel, how you reacted, and what occurred after. Our secrets keep us sick. So it must include your most private and intimate thoughts and feelings. I did the best I could. I would later learn this is the step that causes so many alcoholics to fail. They either do not do it at all or omit embarrassing and private things. It is not easy, but if you want to live, to get your life back, failure is not an option. Next is step five: "Admit to God, myself, and to another human being the exact nature of my wrongs." They brought in people in recovery, many of which had gone through Fellowship Hall to hear our fifth steps. They placed me with an attorney. He had had several years of sobriety and was a nice man. I was so anxious, but he understood. He said that nothing I said would leave the room and that he had been where I was. I finally relaxed and began. The things I was most ashamed of he would laugh at and tell me things he had done, often the very same things. It lasted over two hours. When I finished, I felt great, like I had just unloaded the weight of the world from my shoulders. We all have a dark side. The Native Americans talk about the good dog and the bad dog within. Which one will win today? The one we feed the most. For the first time, I began to realize I was not unique. I had done nothing, hadn't thought anything that many others had not already done or thought, alcoholics or not.

One thing I was so ashamed of was that I used to be ashamed of my parents. They were old enough to be the grandparents of most of my friends. I thought this made me a terrible person. No one ever loved their mom and dad more than I had. They were of an older generation and not stylish. I later realized what a blessing this had been. They had had the wisdom of the ages my friends' parents could not have possessed.

I also believe we all have a knowing, deep down, that there is a God. I grew up during the Vietnam War. I had friends who were in combat. They told me of fellow soldiers whom they had met in boot camp who claimed to be atheist. When they were in foxholes with bullets flying over their heads, mortars going off around them, and friends being blown to pieces, they prayed to God for help. Every one of them. This was why I had no trouble believing in God. I slowly began to think perhaps he would be willing to help me. I had done many stupid things, but I was no criminal. I had been dishonest and manipulative, especially with girls. During my fourth and fifth steps, I was able to see a pattern of behavior develop. From this, I saw my weaknesses and character flaws. Now I was ready for steps six and seven. Step six was "become willing to have God remove all these defects of character," and step seven was "I humbly ask him to remove them." There were woods behind the center with wonderful paths. I took a long walk alone and did my best to do these steps. This was a very private thing, between me and God.

I was feeling better and better. I felt the best I had since before my parents had died. One week each month, they had family week. It happened to fall on my third week there. Alcoholism is a family disease, and the entire family needs treatment. Any alcoholic must have a solid support system after discharge. I was surprised when Jenna showed up. I saw her briefly on Monday morning. I did one counseling session with her on Thursday. Other than that, I did not see her at all. I had heard rumblings that something was going on with her during the week. All of us remained sequestered from any outsiders, so there were days I did not know whether she was there.

The following week, my final one, I was asked to appear in front of the entire treatment team. This was about four days before I was to be discharged. The strange thing about this was that I was the only patient they had done this with. There must have been 150 patients there during my four-week stay. People were constantly being discharged and admitted. I was scared, as I had no idea what was happening. Everyone was talking about it. When I walked into the room, they were all seated in a semicircle. There was a seat for me in front of them in the middle. They sensed I was nervous. So my primary therapist began. She said they were all very pleased with the work I had done there. She then said that I was one they would have had high hopes for if my wife Kathy had still been alive, and I had been going home to her. Then they dropped the bomb.

They said that obviously I was not going home to Kathy, and if I went back to Jenna, I would be drunk in a week. I was stunned. How dare they! This was my personal choice. Besides, I was married to her. They then asked me to compare the two marriages, not the two women. All good marriages have many things in common. I sat there thinking and could not name a single thing. The director spoke up and said, "Harry, this is no marriage! This is tantamount to you going out to a bar, getting drunk, and meeting a woman. Then waking up a week later in Vegas, married to her and not even recalling her name." He continued, "By her admission and yours, the only thing the two of you have done is stay drunk and in bed having sex. This is no marriage." They then asked whether I was aware that she had shown up every morning the prior week drunk, having already consumed a pint of vodka. I asked if they thought she was an alcoholic. I got nothing but silence. I was then told they had tried everything to gain her consent to allow them to admit her as a patient. Since this was strictly an alcohol rehab center, I again asked if they thought her to be an alcoholic. They just looked at one another.

I was becoming very annoyed. I said, "So what in the heck are you trying to tell me?" Finally the psychiatrist spoke. He told me there was no doubt she had a serious alcohol and substance abuse problem. However, every single one of them had met with her and independently determined she had mental issues that were of a much greater concern. I would later understand. The reason they wanted to admit her was so they could put a true diagnosis on her. I now know she was a sociopath. She had no conscience. Of course, they pleaded with me to leave her. They left me with one last thought: What kind of woman would marry a man whom a blind person could see was in serious trouble, not to mention the fact he had just lost his wife of many years, plus his entire family? I had to admit they made a good point. She had drunk with me, drink for drink. Yet I had always known there was something very different about her drinking versus my own. I was drinking because it was like medicine to me. I had lost the power of choice. She was just drinking period. This is the difference between an alcohol problem and alcoholism. They had explained all this my first week. The brain of an alcoholic is different. When we ingest any amount of alcohol, it triggers a biochemical reaction that sets off a compulsion and obsession to drink more and more. This is why when I started, I could not stop. Before I was discharged, I completed my eight steps. I made a list of all people I had harmed in any way and became willing to make amends to them all.

Like an idiot, I went back to Jenna. I was told that to remain sober, I had to change my playmates and playgrounds.

I was also told I must attend ninety AA meetings in ninety days. I did neither. When I walked out of Fellowship Hall, I felt fantastic. I honestly did not believe there was any way I would drink again. I had also been told that, by going through that program, I would have the knowledge of someone with two or three years of sobriety, having only attended AA alone. This went right to my head. My ego to be more precise. Knowledge is not sobriety. I had become what I now call *treatment wise*. I could talk the talk but had no idea how any of it applied to me. I recall attending a meeting, a general discussion meeting, when I had been about thirty-five days sober. I was talking the talk, and afterward a man approached me, asking me to be his sponsor. A sponsor is the person who guides you through every step of sobriety. He had been two years sober. He was blown away when I told him how much time I had been. Much to my amazement, I was drunk a week later, just as they had predicted.

This was 1986, the worst year of my life. I was to go through two more twelve-step recovery centers in a period of the following six months. During this period, I was systematically being robbed blind by Jenna. She told everyone I was an alcoholic and that she was a victim of me. People believed her. Not only did they believe she was innocent but pure as the driven snow. I was to lose everything I had on this earth. I still remember her saying to me, "Everything that was yours is now mine." We had not been married a year. When I married her, she had nothing but the clothes on her back and a sack full of bills, which I paid off. It is hard for me to imagine now why I did not walk away. I did find out, but we'll get to that later.

By the time I got to the third treatment center, I was beginning to find myself and was in a different state of mind. It, too, was a twelve-step program. So there were a lot of redundancies for me. However, it all began to take on more meaning and settle in a deeper place within me. One day I was in a session, and the counselor began describing the biochemical reaction that takes place in our brains once we have a drink. I stopped him and said, "Look, I understand all that. What I do not get is what happens before I take that first drink. At this point there is no reaction. Yet here I am with the full knowledge of my condition and without a shred of evidence to suggest that if I take the drink, it will be different." He pointed to step two on the wall. "Come to believe that a power greater than myself could restore me to sanity." I paused for a moment. Then it hit me. I said to him, "Are you saying I am crazy?" He just looked at me and replied, "What would you call it?" For the first time I became aware of the true meaning of the word "powerless" as it related to alcoholism. I had an epiphany; I understood you could not think your way to sobriety.

The only thing standing between me and that first drink was God. I thought back and remembered there had been days past when I had had no desire to drink. Then it was as if a black cloud came over me, and I was completely powerless to refrain from having that first drink. Once I had had the first, there was no stopping. This scared the daylights out of me. I began to lose all hope. I knew God could but did not think he would help me. My sister, Carolyn, came to visit me. She and her husband were devout Christians. I explained my dilemma regarding my doubts that God would help me. She asked me a question, "What do you think Daddy would say to you if he were here?" I said, "I know he would be very disappointed in me." She replied, "Yes, but do you think he would turn his back on you and refuse to help?" Without hesitation I said, "No way. He would do anything to help me." Carolyn then said, "God is your father in heaven, and his love for you is so much greater than that of any human, including Daddy." Tears began pouring down my cheeks. She said, "Harry, do not ever doubt God's love for you. All you must do is ask for his help from your heart." She begged me to come live with her family and not go back to Jenna. I told her I would think about it. Truthfully I was afraid I might drink again and did not want to bring that into her home and around her children. I had found it virtually impossible to explain alcoholism to any nonalcoholic. I never blamed anyone. How could I? I had a tough time understanding it myself.

A few months prior to this, I had visited Kathy's parents in Johnson City. They were fine people and highly respected all over East Tennessee. I had great respect for her dad, whom we called Paw. However, I had no idea what he thought of me. He was not a person who showed emotions or affection. He was a man whose respect I had always wanted. So one morning I came down for coffee. Eunice said, "Paw wants to talk with you." I thought, "Oh no, I am going to get a lecture." I walked into the den, and we sat down together. To paraphrase, he said the following, "Harry, you know I have nothing against having a drink." Indeed they had cocktail hour every night. It would take a dozen of his drinks to make one of mine. He proceeded to tell me how proud they had been of me. He said, "Harry, you are a well-educated man and have been successful beyond our wildest expectations. You were a fantastic husband to Kathy. People like you when you are not drinking. You just must realize that alcohol does not agree with you and just, by gosh, do not do it." After all those years, I had finally found out what he thought of me. It felt wonderful. But it also left me empty because, by that time, I had come to understand it was not that simple. It was like Nancy Regan's "just say no." That may be great advice for many people, but to alcoholics, it is a joke. Try walking into an AA meeting and telling everyone to just say no. It will bring roaring laughter.

I did return to Greensboro. I had a DUI case pending. I went to court, my license was revoked, and I received ten days in jail. My attorney suggested I do it on the county farm, as opposed to being locked in a jail cell. I must have stood out like a sore thumb in there. When the warden saw I was a college graduate, used good grammar, and was articulate, he asked why I was there. When I told him it was for drunk driving, he shook his head and mumbled something about what a waste of time. He understood that locking an alcoholic up served no one. This place was low security and did not house the hardened criminals. I had never been in jail. I felt like a complete loser being there. I recalled a cliché that said alcoholism will take people from Yale to jail and from Park Avenue to park bench. This seemed to fit me perfectly. No, I did not go to Yale but had attended two large universities. I had ridden down Park Avenue in NYC in limousines many times. I had also found myself on park benches over the past few months. I asked myself how I could have fallen so low in such a short period of time. I had lost everything that was ever important to me. My wife and family, my home, my career, credit, investments, everything. They let me out after only five days.

Believe it or not, I was still with Jenna. But now I was sober and began to assess my situation. I saw for the first time what Jenna had done to me. Back then if you had a high credit rating, banks would send credit cards with large lines of credit in the mail. All you had to do was sign the back and charge something to activate them. Kathy and I would just cut them up but not Jenna. She had intercepted several of these cards and had run up around $75,000 in debt. This was only the tip of the iceberg. One day I received a phone call from a VP at Macy's. She had found a Macy's card somewhere in my house. I did not even know it existed, but Kathy had probably forgotten about it. I had cut all her cards into pieces following her death. Jenna had gone to Macy's and purchased a load of what the VP described as luxury items. In today's money, it would be several thousand dollars. I think it was $2,000 back then. She had forged my dead wife's name on the charge tickets. When they did not get paid, they began searching for Kathy. Obviously they could not find her, but they did find her mom and dad. This is what led them to me. The man begged me to agree to come to court and testify against her. He told me he had been in finance for twenty-five years and had never seen anything like this. He said she was a woman without morals and without a conscious. He was right!

To this day, I still do not know why I did not agree to have her prosecuted. As insane as this sounds now, at that time I blamed myself for everything, including what she had done. I would think if I had not been drinking, none of this would have occurred. I would not have lost my career and everything else. One thing I am not is a hypocrite. I suppose I thought that pointing a finger at her would make me just that. Clearly one thing had nothing to do with the other.

Another thing she did, which broke my heart, was to intercept the death benefit check from the department of social security. It was only $255, but it was not about the amount. She forged my name and cashed it through her little business, which was nothing but a money-laundering deal. She had sold everything she could, none of which was hers. She was a criminal with no morals and no ethics. When I confronted her, she just laughed. It is very hard for me to imagine how I had gotten involved with her, but it was even more difficult to understand why I stayed. Anyone that had even known me before or since, were they told this story would believe I would have put up with this for two seconds. I kept all of it secret. No one knew the truth at that time.

The more I thought about all this, the emptier I felt. I began slipping backward again. On December 31, 1986, I got a pint of vodka and drank it. I was to do a favor for her sister, and it was raining. Her sister and her husband and baby were out of town for Christmas, and she had parked her car in our drive. They were having heating oil delivered but someone had to be there. It was less than a mile away, so I drove her car down. It was a 300ZX sports car. On the way back, I was coming up a little hill and hit the gas pedal. It stuck in full throttle, and I lost control and sideswiped a pickup truck. It was not much of an accident, but the police came, and I was arrested for drunk driving. They were all furious at me. I think I felt as bad as I had following Kathy's funeral. I had stayed away from my family and friends completely. Among her family and friends, I knew I did not have a single person who supported me. I had been sober for several months. I was back to square one.

I finally pulled myself together. I knew I had to get out of there but needed time. I did have a valid driver's license in Tennessee. So I began my search for a career role there. In the interim, I got a job as manager for a men's clothing store. It was mostly business suits. Although it did not pay a lot, it did pay enough to cover the basics. The owner began figuring out what Jenna was all about. He had learned a lot about me and my background. He discovered how successful I had been and how I had lost my wife and my family. He became a good friend. I had not disclosed any of these things to him. He learned through customers, especially doctors. He was Jewish and several doctors went to temple with him. Jenna would drive me to work every morning and pick me up at the end of the day. She had dumped her son with her mom. The only thing she cared about was money.

One weekend she flew to New York with some of her girlfriends. I got paid on Friday, and she was to go grocery shopping because there was not a morsel of food in the house. She did not. Instead she took the money and left for New York. I was going hungry all the time. When she returned she told me she was stressed out and needed a vacation. She took off and went to the beach with her boyfriend. This meant I had to take a cab to and from work. This is when her mom found out what was going on. She hit the roof. She asked why I did not stop her. I told her I had been defined as the bad guy, and she had everyone believing she was a victim. She had refused to give me a phone number to reach her. Although I did not say this to her mom, the truth was I did not care whom she was with or where she was. I then told her mom of the New York trip the week before. She could not believe it. I told her this was just the tip of the iceberg. Jenna's dad, her husband, had recently died of lung cancer. I did not want to tell her more because I knew it could not solve anything and would only upset her more.

I had been interviewing for two different jobs. Both were big money, but one was bigger money. I had the one that was the highest paying lined up. It fell through because the manager was forced to hire an unqualified nurse. Jenna had sabotaged me on the other. Her mom had paid for airline tickets and was trying to help me. Her sister and her mom tried everything to talk sense into her. It finally all came to a head on a Friday night. I told her we needed to talk about a divorce. By this time, she was living with her boyfriend, and I was living alone. Her son was living with her mom. She promised me she would be home after 9:00 p.m. She never showed. I knew where she was and called her girlfriend, which really made her angry. She showed up after midnight and was furious. She said, "I want you out. If you don't get out, then I will get you out." She then left and went back to her boyfriend. I stayed up all night. Kathy's parents had told me they would help me get out. The condition was that it had to be over, not going back and no phone calls trying to patch things up. I made the call first thing on Saturday morning. I was gone in one week. I have not seen Jenna since.

Suddenly I was back in Johnson City, where I had met Kathy, done my undergraduate work, and gotten married, and where her funeral was. I had come full circle. Although I had family there, I felt all alone. They were all very judgmental of me. They criticized everything I did or said. I knew they did not understand, but it still hurt me deeply. I was living in a little one-bedroom efficiency apartment. It had been fifteen years since I had lived there. Every summer Kathy and I would go to the beach with her entire family. It was that time again, but I was not invited. Frankly I do not think I could have taken being there anyway, but it still hurt. I was left alone with floods of memories. When I left there after college, I was on top of the world. Then Kathy and I had a beautiful wedding and had our entire future ahead of us. Now here I sat, with nothing and no one. I had not had a drink in six months. Suddenly I was drunk again. There is no need to try and explain why. There was no way to justify it, and I knew it. I was immediately back to where I had left off, shaking and could not stop.

After a few days, I became scared. I knew if I did not stop, I would need medical help. I called the hospital, and they told me they did not do detox. So I called the police on myself. I explained that if I ran out of booze, I could go into the DTs (delirium tremens) and die. One of the cops was very sympathetic and understanding. He stayed with me. I came up with a plan. He would drive me to the ER where I would present with symptoms that would get the drugs I needed to detox. I knew they would figure it out when they did blood work, and they did. However, by that time. I had been admitted and was in a room. The doctor came in and asked, "Why did you lie to me?" I told him the truth and that I was desperate. He agreed to help me under one condition: after discharge, I would go across the street to the alcohol and drug unit of a psychiatric hospital. I had no intentions of doing that but quickly agreed. The next day two doctors from the psychiatric hospital came to see me. It was not that I did not want help but that I had already been through three rehabs. I just did not see the point. However, the places I had been through were all strictly twelve-step programs. These guys took a different approach. They kept coming back and asking me all these questions. I later discovered they were building a background on me. I was discharged after six days.

Because of the drugs I was on in the hospital, I was high as a kite the entire time, including when I left. I stopped up the street and bought a half gallon of vodka. I checked into a hotel and got wasted. When I awakened the next morning, I just could not believe what I had done to myself. I knew this had to stop. I continued drinking but packed up my little car and arrived at the psychiatric hospital around noon. I sat in the parking lot and finished off the jug of vodka. This was August 25 of 1987. Although I did not know it then, that was the last drink I was to have.

When I walked in there, my soul was dead. My life was over, and I was hopeless. They gave me a couple days to sober up. I had no appetite and suffered terrible insomnia. During this time, they received all my records from the previous treatment centers. They also conducted phone interviews with my family and friends. They met with Kathy's parents personally. They learned two important things: I had had some significant periods of sobriety, even while with Jenna. Secondly and the biggest was that I was no longer with Jenna. Still I was unemployed, destitute, and had no support system. I am sure they figured they had their work cut out for them.

First things first. They had to give me hope. I was brought into the office of the psychiatrist. He said, "Harry, you seem to think you are the only person that alcohol has taken this low. You are not!" He had this very nice ceramic vase sitting on the table between us. He began telling me this story of a man who had lost absolutely everything like me. It sounded even worse than my story. This man had given up and was hopeless. His doctor had a history of performing miracles with similar patients. He was asked if he was willing to do anything and everything asked of him to get better. The doctor asked again, "Are you sure?" He continued, "Even if it sounds crazy to you?" Being desperate, the man said, "Yes." The doctor handed him a vase, like the one in front of me. He instructed the man to throw the vase onto the floor, as hard as he could. The man hesitated but did as he was told. The vase broke into many pieces. The doctor handed him a large paper bag and told him to pick up every single piece. When he had finished, the doctor handed him a large tube of super glue. He told the man to come back in a week, having put it all back together. Before he left, the doctor again reminded him of his pledge to do anything, regardless of how crazy it sounded. Needless to say, it was a huge task, but he got it back together and returned a week later.

The man walked in and produced the vase. He was obviously proud of himself. The doctor took the vase and looked it over, nodding his approval. He then handed it back to the man and instructed him to again throw it to the floor, just like the week before. Now the man really hesitated and thought the doctor was nuts. The doctor again reminded him of his commitment. So reluctantly he threw it onto the floor hard. To his amazement it did not break. The doctor began to explain to the man that the broken vase represented him. He said the vase had broken into many pieces and so was he. He said, "Now we will begin to put you back together, one piece at a time. When we are finished next time, you will not break so easily." The man got it, and so did I. My doctor told me this man had gone on to become a very successful businessman, married with two beautiful children. This was the end of my session. He suggested I return to my room and think about whether I was willing to do anything suggested to me. I got two things from this: I began to gain a little hope and perhaps, more importantly, willingness.

I did return to my room and began to think about my previous efforts to get sober. All had begged me to leave Jenna, and I had not. I was to get a sponsor and I did not. I was also told I must attend AA meetings daily. I had done none of this. There is an old saying, "You can tell an alcoholic, but you cannot tell them much." I had incorrectly believed that, armed with self-knowledge, I could stay sober on my own. To this day, I have never met anyone that could do it alone. A week later I was to attend this group therapy session. We went into this large room where I had not been before. I noticed a second level with a large window overlooking the room. Both the psychiatrist and the psychologist I had been working with were present. They pointed up to the room above, and I saw there was a light on. The medical school was just up the street, so they asked if anyone would mind if a few medical school students observed our session. There were several other patients in there, but none objected. I could not believe it, so I said, "Yes, I absolutely do mind. I am no guinea pig." As I was raising hell about this, the psychologist turned to me and asked why I never wanted to talk about Kathy. I turned to him and said, "What are you talking about? I have no problem talking about her." He said, "Fine, let's talk about her." He would ask a question, and I would begin but quickly reverted to talking about Jenna and all she had done to me. He would say, "We are not talking about Jenna but Kathy." I would begin again, and after a couple of minutes, I would slip back to Jenna. He said, "You do have a problem talking about Kathy." However, it was all very superficial, like things you might read in the obituary of a newspaper. Then the psychiatrist would ask a question about Kathy. I would begin but deviate back to Jenna. This must have happened at least four or five times. Then something happened inside me that I cannot explain to this day. It was like a switch had flipped in my brain, a switch that had been stuck. Suddenly all my walls of defense came crumbling down. The raw grief and pain of her death was staring me in the face. I completely broke down in tears. I went to the floor, and they were holding me, saying, "Let it all out." I have no idea how long this lasted.

When I finally came back to myself, I looked around, and there was no one in the room but me and the two doctors. There was no one upstairs either and never had been. It had all been some kind of diversion trick. They spoke to me very softly and quietly. No one, including me, had ever been able to understand why I was with Jenna nor why I kept returning to her. From the moment I met her, I had ceased grieving over Kathy. Jenna was nothing but a diversion, a wall between me and Kathy. I had focused on her entirely. Subconsciously when these people pleaded with me to get away from her, I could not bear the thought. Deep down I knew it would mean facing those terrible feelings, all alone. Even when I had the spiritual experience that morning where the reality had hit me, I could not leave nor kick her out. Everything was suddenly crystal clear to me. I felt like a coward and that I had brought shame and dishonor to Kathy's memory and to her family. I could not understand why her mom and dad had stood by me. I would later discover that her mom had figured this out. She was a brilliant woman, and she had explained it to her dad. They knew me much better than I had ever suspected. Kathy and I were so young when we met. They had watched us grow up and had understood the depth of love we had for each other. These two men allowed me to sit there for a while. Looking back, this had been a major breakthrough, and I was now standing at a crossroads.

I finally stood and walked back to my room. I fell to my knees in tears and began to pray: "God, you took away my mom and dad. You took away my brother and my wife and left me here a hopeless alcoholic. Please either help me or let me die, and I really do not care which." I truly did not. I had prayed many times, but this time my prayers came from my soul, deep within my heart. Suddenly I felt a peace come over me, one I had not felt for many years. This was the turning point. After this a series of coincidences began occurring in my life, every day. They were not big things but just enough to let me know I was not alone, that God was with me constantly. After all these years, that day remains the most important and powerful one in my life.

Chapter 8

Rebuilding My Life

I was to remain there for thirty days. Their next goal for me was finding a long-term care place for me to go when discharged. I did not argue. I knew I needed a support system and professional help to guide me the rest of the way into quality sobriety. I was aware they were referring patients to local halfway houses. I overheard a conversation regarding me. Someone suggested to one of my doctors that perhaps I should go to one of these houses. He replied, "No way. Harry would be running the place in a week." He needs to be around his own kind. The next day they told me about the MARR program in Atlanta. It was originally designed for doctors and medical professionals. It was now for all professionals. I said fine, but I had no insurance and no money. They informed me they had a plan. The following day I was asked to come down to this boardroom in a part of the building I had never been in. When I walked in, I was stunned to see Kathy's mom and dad sitting there with my two doctors. I had figured they never wanted to see me again after they had helped me get out of Greensboro, and I got drunk. I learned they had been involved the entire time and had followed my progress through my entire stay there. I was amazed to hear that they were willing to put up the money to get me into MARR. I became very emotional, and I do not think I was ever more humbled. I agreed to pay them back (and did two years later). I was discharged two days later. It was late in the day, which meant I would have to stay in a hotel one night. I left feeling great, better than I had felt in years.

When I crossed the state line into Georgia, I spotted a Days Inn. To my amazement I considered getting just a pint of vodka. I did not, but the fact I had considered it scared me to death. I think it was God, reminding me I had a long way to go. I also knew that when it came to booze, I could never trust myself. This fear kept me focused on my recovery and kept me willing to do anything. I would later learn you cannot stay sober on fear. The only thing that could get me drunk was me. Many people would call my stays in the previous treatment centers failures. I do not because they did their job. I did not do mine. Still I had learned so much. I would be discharged feeling great and thinking there was no way I would drink again. Friends would approach me asking how I was doing with the drinking thing. I would reply, "Fine." They would ask if I missed it, and I would say, "Nah." I was not so much lying to them but to myself. In my intellect, I would think that considering all the hell alcohol had put me through, there could be no way I would want to drink again. Yet deep down, another drink was all I wanted. This is the epitome of alcoholism. It is also the root of self-honesty. Wanting another drink is normal for an alcoholic, despite how illogical it may seem. Saying it is not a desire is the heart of denial. Alcoholism is called a disease of denial. This was my first hard lesson in getting honest with myself.

I arrived at MARR. I was placed in a house with seven other men. There was another house up the street with another eight men. This made up our treatment community. There were doctors, lawyers, business executives, and even an Episcopal priest. This took away my denials that, due to my education and levels of success, I could not be an alcoholic. Some of these men made me look like a failure. I had certainly met my match, and this interested me. We ate, slept, and breathed recovery. This was seven days a week and twenty-four hours a day. We were in either private or group sessions every day. We attended AA meetings every night and church on Sundays. The rules were very strict. Breaking one meant immediate discharge. I also had to sign an agreement that I would do anything asked of me. I did not hesitate. I knew this was my last chance. It was do or die. I had run out of options.

My first private session was with Dr. Eddy, a woman. My appointment was early in the morning. I walked on a small path, a shortcut, through the woods to get there. I was greeted by the receptionist and led into an office. I was instructed to take a seat on this large sofa. I remember sinking down so low I felt trapped. She arrived a couple minutes late and took a chair in front of me. She wasted no time getting to it. She told me she had an important question for me. She then paused and looked directly into my eyes. And it felt like she was looking through me. Then she asked, "What is it that you want?" I was silent. She asked again, "What do you want out of your life?" I just sat there thinking, and she said nothing. I finally replied and said, "I just want to be happy." She smiled and told me this was a good answer. I had never thought about this before.

When I was young, I thought having a good education, a good job, lots of money, a good wife, a home, etc. would bring me happiness. I had achieved all those things before Kathy died but was not at peace or happy inside myself. I explained all this to her. These things only brought temporary happiness. The new always wore off. I recalled being so happy the day we moved into our new home, but a year later it was just a house. I had bought new cars and was over the moon with them, but six months later they were just transportation. She began to explain that all these things were outside of me. There was nothing wrong with wanting and obtaining them. The problem was the fact I thought they would make me happy. It comes down to how we hold these things within ourselves. She said no one will ever find true happiness outside themselves. If we are not first happy within, falling in love with someone will not do any more than a new car or house. It will only provide temporary happiness. Finding happiness became my goal in life. It still is. They would take me on a journey to find inner peace.

The next plan for my treatment was to take me through the grief process. Then they wanted me to work through the anger and resentment I had with Jenna. For me to find the happiness I sought, I first had to clean house. Anger and resentment are poison to the soul. They would also drive me backward, into the bottle. Since I was a little boy, I had always had a hot temper. However, give me five minutes, and I was done with it. But this was not happening with my anger over Jenna. I have shared several things she did to me, but there was so much more. It had not stopped when I left. I had liquidated two CDs, and the bank had sent the checks in error to her. At the time I was so broke I could not even buy a soda, and she had my money. It was several thousand dollars. I was fuming!

I was in a group session one afternoon with the men in my house. I described some of the vile things she had done to me. Everyone was shocked. I was ranting and raving when Dr. Price stopped me. He was a psychiatrist who had ten years in recovery and had gone through MARR. He asked me who had placed the gun to my head and forced me to marry her. Of course, I said, "No one." He then asked how many people tried to talk me out of it. I had to tell him, "It was pretty much everyone." Then he asked how many tried to get me away from her after the marriage. Again I said every one of my family members and friends. He then used this analogy: What if a man came here from another planet and knew nothing about the nature of fire? This man walked to a gas stove with the fire on and placed his hand in it. People would explain this logically, saying he just did not understand fire. However, what if he continues to go back, day after day, placing his hand in the fire? He has now burned all the skin off his hands down to the bones. Now the man is very angry at the fire. Where is the logic in that? Fire is hot. That is its nature. It can burn you or cook your food. Some people are evil. That is their nature. He said Jenna could have great sex with me, but like the fire, she burned me badly. This was her nature.

He said, "Harry, you kept going back and placing your hand in the same fire and expecting different results. Now you are angry at the fire." I got it. He then gave me three assignments: First I was to meditate on what we had just discussed. Second I was to call her and make amends to her for everything I had done. Third and finally I was to pray for her daily for the next thirty days. I thought he was mad! Are you kidding me? I had someone suggest that I hire a hit man, and you want me to pray for her. I told him he needed help. He then reminded me of the contract I had signed, agreeing to do whatever I was told.

I just did not know if I could do these things. I did go back to my room and spend time thinking about what had been said. I had to admit he was dead on target. I had placed myself in the position. I had gone from my mom and dad to Kathy. I had never encountered a single person like her, before or since. I was naive and trusted everyone. I also knew that being drunk had placed me into darkness. There was no way I would have gotten involved with her, much less marry her, had I been sober. However, you simply cannot *unfire* a gun or diffuse a bomb after it has gone off. It took me a couple of days to get the nerve to call her, but I did. The directions I had been given were that I was only to make amends to her to clean my side of the street. I could not say, "Yes, but look at what you did to me." She would have to carry that load, not me. When I think back on that day, I have to laugh; I told her I was calling to make amends to her. I told her I was sorry for marrying her. I had told her I was over Kathy's death and clearly was not. I had lied to her and to myself. I also told her I was sorry for being an alcoholic, which had precluded me from being a good husband. She had nothing to say in response. It would be thirty years before she apologized for what she had done to me. I do not believe she is sorry at all, but that is her problem, not mine. After this I had to admit it did feel good. I felt a lot lighter. Praying for her was a real challenge initially. In the beginning my prayers went something like, "God, please help that bitch."

As the days passed, something inside me began changing. Within two weeks my anger was gone. By the end of the month, I was truly praying for her. She had not changed, but I had. I just could not believe it. To this day, I still have no anger nor resentment against her. Occasionally I will have a memory slip through, and I find myself getting angry, but I just go back and pray for her. I had just learned a powerful life lesson. It was profound; prayer can change one's heart. I also know it can change others, but regardless, it changes me.

I felt a lot of guilt regarding the deaths of my family. I felt I should have been there more for my mom and dad. When Kathy was suffering, I had wished God would take her. It was so painful to see her in agony and feel powerless to do anything about it. After she passed I was angry at her for leaving me. My brother had had heart problems since he was a kid. Still he drank and smoked. I had tried to convince him to stop but was not successful. I felt it was my fault. I now know that these feelings, though irrational, are normal. Back then I had no way to know any of this. Dr. Price helped me walk through it all. I had been overwhelmed with these feelings.

Following my dad's death, we had to place my mom in a nursing home. This was eating me alive. It took time for me to process all of this. I had a lot of help, both in group sessions and private ones. I had not dealt with any of the grief. I just poured alcohol on it. I also discovered I had used Jenna as a diversion. Overall it made me feel like a bad person, not a man but a coward. Now that I was clean and sober, my feelings were so intense. I suddenly recalled so many things I should have done. Then Dr. Price told me something I never forgot; he said, "Feelings are neither right nor wrong—they just are. Feelings may or may not be based in reality." I do not know why, but this seemed to help me. It lifted the weight of the baggage I was carrying. He also explained that most of what I was feeling was completely normal. He shared several stories of others who had lost loved ones. He pointed out that no one is perfect, and we all make mistakes. The issue is what we do about our mistakes. Do we face them and accept responsibility for them? If we do, we learn and evolve as people. If we do not hold ourselves accountable, we digress as human beings. Plus we are likely to repeat the same mistakes over and over.

My biggest worry was how I could make amends to someone who had died. My largest regrets were due to things I had done while married to Kathy. I traveled a lot and was guilty of infidelity. She was not a highly sexual person. Although I was very discreet, I felt strongly that she knew. When I was with Jenna and discovered she was out with other men, it hurt. I would think, "Oh my God. Is this how I made Kathy feel?" I knew I had been with a few other women and always when I was drunk. I also knew that was no excuse. My drinking had caused several problems between me and Kathy. I had embarrassed her and felt awful about it. I shared all of this with Dr. Price. His solution was to have me write a long letter to Kathy, baring my soul. I reluctantly agreed. It took a couple of weeks for me to complete the letter. It was cathartic but very painful for me. I only saw Dr. Price one or two days a week.

On one of those days, he led a group session for our treatment community. There were about fifteen men, plus Dr. Price. When he arrived I told him I had completed the letter to Kathy. When everyone was seated, he dropped the bomb on me. He asked me to read it aloud in the group. To say I was stunned was the understatement of all time. Initially I flat refused. This was not only private but intimate. So he brought up my contract, which I saw as dirty pool. He then asked a question: "Harry, I have asked you to do several things you did not want to do, but you did. Think about the results you got from each." He had me there. So I finally pulled out the letter and slowly began to read.

I wish I had kept it but did not. It was six pages, single spaced. By the time I got through the first page, I was in tears. I continued reading and never looked up. When I had finally finished, I did look up and around the room. Every single man in that room, including Dr. Price, was in tears. No one said a word. I just sat there totally drained. Had I known he would ask me to read this in group, the letter would have been very different. I had not expected anyone to hear it, not even Dr. Price. Normally the sessions would last ninety minutes. Although it had started just under an hour before, he ended the session for the day. When we all stood and the guys were leaving, Dr. Price took me by the arm and hugged me. Then he told me something I have never forgotten. He said, "Harry, I want you to know that you are a quality person." It might sound arrogant for me to say this, but at the time I really needed to hear that. I had nothing but the greatest respect for him and knew he was not prone to offering compliments. I had felt so bad about myself that I felt lifted in a big way. Later when I was with the other men, every single one came to me and told me how deeply moved they were. They even began treating me differently. Not better nor worse, just differently. They were still talking about that day until we were discharged. Dr. Price told me my sharing had opened these men to getting honest about their own feelings. He said this is a big reason why group therapy is so effective.

I had made a good start but still had a distance to go. We had to attend AA meetings every night. Suddenly a big issue arose with me. I was not talking, not sharing in the meetings. When I had first been discharged from the three treatment centers, I would attend meetings. You could not shut me up. However, it was all coming from my head, from my intellect. I had not stayed sober either. Looking back, I just did not know how to talk from my heart, not in situations like that. Over the years, research has shown that when a person begins drinking or using drugs, they cease maturing emotionally. As years pass we completely lose ourselves. I had studied AA and its history like a course in college. I had no clue how it connected to my inner self. I thought I was my brain and lived in my intellect. I later discovered that many people live this way, not just alcoholics. We go through life deaf, blind, and dumb with regard to our spiritual genome. Back in the 1960s, a lot of young people used LSD to find themselves and get answers. All of us, at some point in our lives, search for truth. Alcohol and drugs only cut us off from our inner selves. Anyway I somehow arrived at the conclusion that all this bull that was coming out of me was of no value to my sobriety or to anyone else. I was terrified to open up in a room full of strangers.

This continued for weeks, and my therapists were all over me. I could speak openly in group and in my one-on-one sessions. I had also seen the great benefits derived from it. They finally gave me an ultimatum. Finally I was in a meeting one night and decided this was it. The time was running out, so I raised my hand and was called on. I was scared to death but began talking about how I felt regarding the topic being discussed. I even revealed the fear I had on the issue being talked about. I only spoke for four or five minutes. When the meeting closed, I had several people approach me and tell me how touched they were at what I had shared. I was blown away. From that evening forward, I never had an issue sharing from my heart. What I discovered was that my honesty and the honesty of others served everyone. This is why AA is so effective. I discovered I was not unique and never alone in how I felt. Later, I learned that this was not only true with alcoholics but all people. We need each other in life. Looking back, this was the beginning of my self-discovery. I was just beginning to find out who I was. I was not the person I thought I was. It was the beginning of finding my inner self.

The most critical factor for long-term sobriety lies in self-honesty. Many alcoholics never stay sober. Even those who appear to be doing everything right. There is a line in the AA big book that says there are those, too, who seem to be constitutionally incapable of being honest with themselves. Their chances are less than average. Keeping secrets will keep you sick. Over time even small secrets grow and evolve into major issues. I had never considered myself a dishonest person. I was not a thief nor a criminal.

Every Wednesday afternoon we had what was called "Big Group." All professionals, men and women, attended. There were fifty or sixty people in there. Some had just been admitted, and others had from two to five years of sobriety. The chairs were arranged in a big circle. Donnie Brown, who was the founder of MARR and the director, ran this group. It was very confrontational. If anyone got a clue you were hiding something, they would call you out.

The rest of the group would attack you like vultures. One Wednesday I arrived early and took a seat. Donnie walked in. Although most every seat was empty, he came and sat beside me. He sounded like an old Southern Baptist preacher. He looked at me and said, "Harry, are you honest?" This scared me to death. I replied, "Yes, I think I am pretty honest." I was certain he was going to throw me to the wolves that day. He did not, but I began thinking about it. No, I was not a thief, but I was very dishonest with myself. From that day I began a lifelong process of peeling back the layers of the onion to discover my true nature. I was more afraid of being called out in that group than working through my layers of dishonesty. I soon learned this would become a lifelong process.

The next major issue to be addressed was fear. I grew up in a time when real men were not afraid. Even if they were, they did not admit it. By attending all the small and large group sessions, I soon learned the fallacy of that belief. Every man there was full of fear. Many of these men were major figures, and two had names you might recognize if I mentioned them. By witnessing their fear, my walls started crumbling, and I could look at my own. By this time, I had found a sponsor. His name is Bob, and we are close to this very day. Bob knew a lot about fear. He had served two tours in Vietnam as a special forces team member. The Green Berets! When I left North Carolina, I had a DUI case pending for the last time I was caught.

I was terrified to face it. Not only would it be my fourth conviction, but I was also charged for driving when my license was revoked. I figured they would lock me up and throw away the key. I also knew I was technically a fugitive from justice. I told Bob the entire story. I will never forget his response. He did not judge me and did not attempt to tell me what to do. He said, "Harry, the one thing I have learned in life is a fact that never changes. That is, if you are to be happy and at peace, you will have to face your greatest fears." It hit me hard. Deep down I knew he spoke the truth, even then. I had planned to acquire another fake license. My friend and attorney even went to a cemetery and got a name off a tombstone. In the end, I just could not do it. I did return to face the music but a couple years later. I received no jail time. The judge called all my time in treatment "time served." There were two carloads of people with me. They stood up in court for me. Of course this was an external type of fear.

Internally fear can manifest in many forms: anger, rage, hatred, violence, crime, envy, jealousy, and greed. And my alcoholism was a way to handle fear. I had to look within at all of these. For example, I would attend meetings and find myself angry at someone. The question became, Why? Most often it was because I saw something in them that I disliked in myself. On one occasion, there was a man who was indeed creating problems. He was annoying everyone. One day I had had enough and confronted him in the meeting. I really lowered the boom on him. What I said was all true. He knew it, and so did everyone else. Afterward people were thanking me, but I did not feel good about it. I had humiliated him. What I should have done was take him aside and done it in private. Plus I did it out of anger. So I had to call him and make amends. I honestly did not like him, so making amends was difficult. I did call and told him I took nothing back I had said but apologized for the way I had done it. He accepted my apology and much later thanked me for calling him out.

This, too, would become a lifelong process. Any emotion I felt that was fear based, I would look within myself. This created a domino effect. I had also learned that I was powerless over people, places, and things. The only power I possessed was over my own actions and choices. I am not responsible for what you think of me. I had spent my entire life worrying what others thought of me. Now my only concern was what God thought of me and what I thought of myself. I could not believe the freedom I found in this ideology. Although I had lost everything, I had felt this freedom. I recalled a song from my teen years, performed by the late Janis Joplin. One of the lyrics was, "Freedom's just another word for nothin' left to lose." That line was so very true and described me perfectly at that time. Anything that occurred that upset me in some way, I looked within. What part, if any, had I played in it? My sole responsibility was to keep my side of the street clean. I had no power over anyone else's actions. From all these exercises, I developed a personal philosophy that I still adhere to today: "If I am not the problem, then I have no solution." Practicing this always holds me accountable for everything I do or say. I do not like the actions of many people, but neither am I responsible for them. This does not preclude me from trying to help others, and I do. I admit I have crossed the line a couple of times by getting too involved with the decisions and choices of others. It backfires on me every time. My job in helping others is not telling them what to do or trying to fix them. It is simple: I share my own experience, strength, and hope with others. People must make their own choices.

Another major issue I had to deal with was living in the past. One of AA's big mottos is "one day at a time." Initially I thought it was just about not drinking one day at a time. Anyone can stop for a day, but telling an alcoholic they can never drink again is overwhelming. I soon discovered that one day at a time was much more. It was about living in the now. Yesterday is gone forever. Tomorrow never comes because when tomorrow arrives, it will be today. Now is all we have. We all can only have 100 percent of energy in each moment. If we expend say 70 percent of it thinking about the past, we have very little remaining for the present. I had to let go of the past. Doing my ninth step of making amends to everyone helped. My biggest challenge was letting go of my feeling that, by marrying Jenna, I had brought shame and dishonor to Kathy's memory as well as to her family and mine. It would be years before I finally cut loose of this. However, it was then pointed out that I had to make an even bigger amend—that being to myself. I had not even considered that. This, too, would take time. As I was finally able to begin leaving the past, I switched my focus to my future. Guilt and shame had dominated my feelings when I lived in the past. Now it was fear that took over. How could I ever rebuild my career, my financial portfolio, etc.?

Fear of the unknown produces anxiety for most everyone. As I reflected on my life, I had never really lived in the present. It was always, "When I complete this, or I get that, I will be happy." Of course I never got enough of anything. Regardless of how much success I had found, and I had found a lot, I would compare myself to someone else and end up feeling like a failure. When Kathy and I got our first home, we were so excited. Then I noticed it was one of the smallest homes in the neighborhood. It had become a bad habit. It did produce a lot of ambition in me, but I had twisted it. I was doing everything for the wrong reasons. Then Dr. Price introduced me to a new philosophy: Only compare myself to myself, not others. He said, "Harry, look where you came from, the son of a coal miner, living in Appalachia. You ended up riding in limousines on Park Avenue in New York City." He said, "To coin a phrase, 'You have come a long way, baby.'" Furthermore he told me that I would always find greater and lesser people than myself. Just do your best and leave the results to God—period. Then the subject also included an attitude of gratitude. Be grateful for what you have today. Life can change in an instant. Maintaining an attitude of gratitude and living in the present was not like flipping a switch and saying, "Yes, I will do this." Old habits are hard to break. He told me I would need to monitor my thoughts constantly.

These things, along with most others, would take a lifetime to accomplish. All these years later, I can tell you I have never mastered them, but I sure have come a long way, baby. I recall a business associate I did a lot of work with. He was in management with a client company of mine. We had become good friends. He was then a vibrant and very successful middle-aged man. One night he had to get out of bed to go urinate. He was half asleep, the room was dark, and he tripped, falling head first into the wall. He went down and never got up. He had broken his neck and was left paralyzed. A few weeks later, another friend and I went to visit him at the Shepherd Center in Atlanta. He was seated in one of those mechanical wheelchairs. He could only move a few fingers to operate the chair. He was smiling and so grateful he could move his fingers. This just tore me and my friend Jimmy to pieces. We saw countless other patients there in basically the same condition. I thought of how many times I had awakened at night in similar circumstances. It could have happened to me or any of us so easily. He did improve some, but his life was changed forever. Every time I find myself getting down, I think of him. I have absolutely nothing to complain about. Every time I complain about something, I think of him and am almost ashamed of myself.

Chapter 9

AA

I WAS BEING given tools to live by. None of these things had anything to do with alcoholism. They were about living. I would later discover that none of these tools were designed for alcoholics. AA contains nothing new. The founders just organized it into steps that made is simple for alcoholics to follow. These principles have been around since the beginning of mankind. Unfortunately they have become lost from one generation to another, then rediscovered by a few spiritually minded individuals. I became aware that I was being born again into a new life. A new life with God at the helm. Absolutely everything took on a new meaning. I had to reexamine everything I had believed and thought. The bottom line was that I was happy, the happiest I had been since I was a little boy. I felt childlike at times. Yes I was financially broke, unemployed, and destitute but happy. How could this be? I somehow understood I was in God's hands and trusted in his will for me.

During my time at MARR, I spent thirty days working at a walk-in treatment center for street drunks. This was referred to as mirror imaging. On the one hand, I had almost nothing in common with these people, at least on the exterior. However, as I sat in their group sessions, I quickly began to see I had everything in common with them. We all suffered from the same disease, yes, but it was much more than that. We had the same fears, feelings, and concerns. We were all just human beings. This was the beginning of my learning not to judge people. Some of these people were drug addicts, dealers, and criminals. I certainly did not approve of their behavior. This is where I began to learn of the importance of acceptance. To accept their bad behavior did not mean I agreed with it on any level. Evil exists in the world, always has and always will. We never know where a person is on their life journey. People thought I was crazy when I married Jenna. I was! However, in retrospect, it served a purpose.

I am married today with a wonderful relationship, and I know I am a much better husband than I would have been. I have much more appreciation for having an honest woman, one whom I trust with my life, as a result of the time I spent with Jenna. The practice of acceptance is an avenue to inner peace. Nothing in God's world happens by mistake. We must accept that things are unfolding exactly as they should, at any point in time. Many of us must first travel a tough road before we find the right path. Who among us would want to be defined by our lowest moment? I would hate to be defined by the man I was in 1986. But had I not lived through 1986, I would not have found the path that has led to where I am today.

There was nothing complicated about the program for recovery. We often spoke of using the KISS principle, "Keep it simple, stupid!" It came down to practicing all these principles in every aspect of our lives. I begin my day by asking God to guide me in everything I think, say, and do. During the day, I would apply every tool I had been given. Thank God, I did not have to do it perfectly. This is why we refer to it as "practicing these principles in all our affairs." At the end of each day, I give thanks and reflect on the day. When I did something wrong or hurt someone, I admitted it. When necessary I immediately made amends. This kept me clean, day by day. Last, I helped others whenever the opportunity arose. Here again this had nothing to do with alcoholism. It had to do with living a simple and spiritual life.

I had built a support system of friends. I had become best friends with John. When we finished the ninety-day mark in MARR, which was 120 days of sobriety, we were moved to what they called three-quarter houses. At this point we were told to get jobs. The jobs could not be related to our professions. So we had doctors working in car washes and similar roles. When Kathy and I first got married, she could not find a job. I took a part-time job in a shoe store to earn extra money. So I found a job in a shoe store in Buckhead. I also got my friend John a job there. These jobs were humbling for all of us. However, John had worked in open-heart surgery at Baptist Hospital, earning huge money. When customers came in, especially surgeons, and recognized him, he had to be embarrassed. He never showed it though.

The idea was not to just humble us but to keep our entire focus on our recovery. We had to continue looking into the mirror. A professional role or a relationship with the opposite sex would create chaos internally. It would certainly split our focus. All of us had attended countless numbers of AA meetings, but most had been in AA clubhouses. There we found mostly early sobriety. In some cases, it felt like the blind leading the blind. There was another cliché that said, "Always stick with the winners." If someone in our treatment community was not taking this seriously, we avoided them. I felt they were poison to me. We have all seen kids get mixed up with the wrong crowd, doing drugs, stealing, etc. What happens is those behaviors soon become normal, and a previously good kid is in jail. With alcoholism, it is a matter of life and death. So when we were moved to another house in another area of the city, we found new meetings.

One of these, "The Tucker Group," quickly became my home group. There was some early sobriety there, like myself at the time, but there were a lot of long-term sobrieties.

It was a large meeting, but following the initial readings, we broke up into small discussion groups. I loved it because I felt more comfortable opening up in these smaller groups, and it was clear that others did too. I met men with twenty and thirty years of sobriety. They had great careers, homes, and families. This gave me hope. When I arrived in Atlanta, I had no significant hope. It became a question of this: if these men could do it, then perhaps so could I. They embraced me and became my guides. This meeting was held on Monday night and on Friday night.

Initially I was still living in MARR housing. Then something occurred that redirected my path. One Saturday night, John and I had attended a meeting at the NABA clubhouse. When I was doing my mirror imaging, I worked with this woman from the female group of MARR. We called them the "marr-ettes." As we were leaving NABA, I spotted her and another woman. I said hello. We then decided to go to a movie at Northlake Mall. When we arrived and were standing in line for tickets, I looked up and there were these two women. So the four of us went in and watched the movie. Afterward we went our separate ways.

The following Wednesday, we were in "Big Group." I sensed that something was up. Donnie Brown gave me a hard look. Here is basically what had happened: this woman had told some of the other women in her group that she was sleeping with me. She told them she and her friend had met John and I and gone to the movies. It was all lies, but Dr. Eddy believed her. I had known young boys to do this, to claim they had had sex with a girl but had never known a girl to do it. They kicked all four of us out. I was very upset because I knew I was innocent, and my friend John did not even know these women. We had to act and began searching for an apartment. I was invited to live with my sponsor, Bob, for a week or two. We rented an apartment by the NABA club. We rented a truck and went to North Carolina where I had stored furniture and my belongings. It took two weeks to accomplish all of this. I was then called to appear before the treatment team. I again professed my innocence. The crazy thing was that I had no interest whatsoever in women at that time. This was the source of my pain, and I told them this. I think the men believed me. They told me they were impressed that I had not gone back to drinking, a thought that had not entered my mind.

They invited both John and I to move back in, but we both declined. We had signed a lease and had just finished setting up our apartment. The only thing that would change was my place of residence. I would continue attending my sessions at MARR and would remain under their supervision. This was the acid test for me. I had been under tight supervision, 24-7, for seven months. I knew I must use every tool I had been given in every aspect of my life. I continued to do the same things I had been doing.

I went to meetings daily, went to church on Sundays, and worked with my sponsor.

Bob was pure AA sober, having never gone through a treatment center. In some ways, we were very different but not where it counted. He could always see through me and reach the core of the matter. He is still my sponsor to this day, but our relationship has changed. He is more like family, like my brother. Bob was a mentor, but I found several mentors. There is simply no replacement for experience. I had always had older men to guide and coach me. Even in college I had roommates who were four or five years older. When you are nineteen and living with a person who is twenty-three or twenty-four, that is a big deal. They had been in the military and seen many things. The man who hired me in my first medical job, Dick Holeman, remained my mentor until his death at ninety-four, just a few years ago. His daughter and I are very close friends to this day. So I used the same strategy in my recovery. I found men at my home group with twenty-five to thirty years of sobriety and stuck with them. Bob had three years of sobriety when we met. He kept me close to the disease. These older men helped me with the larger picture. I could see a future far beyond where I was.

Let go and let God! I had seen and heard this a million times. It had just never sunken in. For this was not about believing in God, which I did. It was about trusting in God and his will for me. Giving up control of outcomes was just not in my basic makeup. It went against everything I had ever been taught. I was about, "Get out there and make it happen." When I first heard the concept of "just do your best and leave the results to God," it sounded great. Living this was a very different matter. I was on autopilot and naturally attempted to control everything. Jesus had asked the question of whether worry has ever added a single thing to anyone's life. The obvious answer is no. Trying to control everything invariably produces worry and fear. This was exactly what I did not want. This practice became a lifelong project for me. When I am working on a business deal, it is still difficult for me to avoid trying to control the outcome. I discovered every time I found myself deeply invested in outcomes, I had set myself up for a fall. When I just gave it my very best and told myself it would work out as it was supposed to, I won many times. But even when I lost, I was not devastated. I just accepted it as God's will.

I truly wish I could tell you that I have mastered this practice, but I have not. But I have come a long way, baby. I find I must consciously remind myself to let go and let God. I find it depends on where I am spiritually at the time. When I am successful in this practice, it is the ultimate in maintaining inner peace and happiness.

Chapter 10

New Career and New Marriage

By this time, I was approaching my one-year anniversary of sobriety. One year is a big deal, a hallmark. It does not mean you are out of danger. I have seen many people celebrate a year and go back out drinking a month later. If we have not completed building a solid foundation of practicing all the principles in all our affairs, we are not likely to remain sober. Fortunately I had, and had also faced all my issues. Now it was time for me to begin rebuilding a career. The treatment team gave me the thumbs up to do so. I continued working at the shoe store. When I first went there, I was honest with them. They understood. John and I had done a good job for them, and they would become a place that employed many MARR people over the years. When I had an interview, they did not object. I did go on a few interviews. The feedback was that I was overqualified, had earned too much money, and had been in management. I also visited several search firms. I was not impressed with any of them.

Then I found one in Dunwoody that impressed me very much. The owners were a husband-and-wife team, both from the medical device industry. The husband had a similar background to mine. We had even worked for the same company, at different times. I was meeting with the wife, and she shared with me that he had suffered a bad heart attack. He was in the hospital, and they could not get him down. He was working jobs. He then suffered a bad stroke, which left him without speech. He was not only out, but it was unlikely he would ever work again. She approached me about joining her team. I was flattered but said, "No thanks." Frankly not only had I never thought this was something I might like to do, but I did not even like most of the people in that arena. I had had my time wasted, been lied to, and had things misrepresented. I went home and told John about it. I treated it as a joke, but he said nothing.

A couple days later, we went to our meeting, the Friday night meeting at Tucker. As always we broke into small groups. I had met a young woman there named Maggie. She was always in the same group as me. I had always been naive where women were concerned. A woman could be in love with me, and I would not notice. Plus at this time, I had absolutely zero interest in dating. I did not even seem to have any sex drive. I had talked about Kathy's death and the tragedy that followed with Jenna. When the meeting broke up, I walked out into the hallway and was waiting for John. Maggie followed me out and approached me. She asked me when we were going to go out together. It caught me completely off guard. I said something like, "I will have to get back to you on that. I must go now. John is waiting on me." And then I took off like a scared cat. I am certain that it would have been amusing to have been a fly on the wall. On the way home, I told John what had just happened. He did not say a word. During this entire period, I had been praying morning and night for God to help me find what I *needed*. I was careful not to ask for what I wanted. I was really trying to turn my life and will over to God. John was aware of this, and he was doing much the same thing.

When we arrived home that evening, he said he had something to discuss with me. We sat down in the living room. He looked at me and said, "Harry, you are full of shit." I was taken back. I asked what he was talking about. He said, "You have been telling me about praying morning and night for God to help you find what you need. God has placed two things in front of you, and you have turned your nose up at both." He said he had an older brother in executive search, and he earned a great living. He said, "Harry, I love my brother, but you could run circles around him." He asked why I was so opposed to it. I explained my experiences of having been manipulated and lied to, etc. He said, "Then why don't you go do it the way you think it should be done? There is no law that a person must be dishonest and unethical to do this job or any other." I had to admit, he had a point.

Harry & Maggie

Then he took off about Maggie. He said, "Harry, she is a nice girl. She is not asking you to get married. She just likes you and wants to spend some time with you." We had both come from a very confrontational treatment program. I just never expected this from John. I was not happy about it. I went to my room and closed the door. I began to think about everything he had said to me. The big point was that I was really asking God for what I wanted, at least on a subconscious level. I reluctantly conceded to myself that he was right. I was not doing it intentionally, but old habits are hard to break. I went into my prayers that night and asked God if this was true. Immediately the answer came back as yes. I thought about it nonstop that weekend.

On Monday I called the search firm and told TJ, the owner, I would like to come back and discuss the matter with her. I decided I was going to tell her the truth of what had happened in my life, that I was in recovery and had commitments that would make it necessary to leave the office occasionally. I figured if this was God's will, it would not be an issue. The following day I met with her. I did tell her the truth, and she did not flinch. She told me of a plan to franchise the business, to open regional offices nationally. She asked for my help. She said we would open a separate cooperation to organize this under. She had an invalid husband and small child and was not able to travel. I would do the work and, in return, receive 50 percent share in the new company. I walked out that day feeling very excited.

That night I called Maggie and scheduled a date for the following Sunday. I arrived at her apartment around 1:00 p.m. We went to a movie and afterward to an early dinner. We arrived back at her place around six o'clock. We began talking, and the next time I looked at my watch, it was 2:00 a.m. We had told each other our life stories. I mean very private and personal things. It was as if we had known each other in a past life and were just bringing each other up to date on what had happened so far in this life. I had to leave because I was starting my new job that day. When I awakened that morning, I was in shock that I had told her all those things. But she had also told me many things. I went to work that day, and it went very well. I had to be trained first. That night we went to our meeting, as it was Monday night. I saw Maggie the minute I walked in. She came to me and said, "I really had a wonderful time with you." I replied, "So did I, but I cannot believe I told you all those things." She then said, "You told me—look at what I told you." We just laughed.

From that time to this very day, we have never been apart. I am still in the same business too. Now here is the moral of the story. I did not want either one of those things. Left to my own devices, neither would have occurred. God used John as an instrument to awaken me. He did just that. How do any of us know what is good for us? Maggie and I have a marriage that was made in heaven. The business turned out to be perfect for me and for many reasons. I just did not understand all of this at the time.

During the next year, Maggie and I would bond together like glue. We had no secrets. Whatever we did not disclose to each other on our first date, we would finish telling one another over the following weeks. Neither of us had anything, but she came from a wealthy family. She had grown up on Philadelphia's Main Line. She had never been married before and was four years younger than me. She had been in a couple of long-term relationships, neither of which her dad approved of. Her mom had died when she was eleven years old. She worshipped her dad. He was a self-made man and was the same age as my parents had been. In the beginning, I did not fall in love with Maggie, but I sure did fall in *like* with her. We became best friends almost immediately. Then one day, I just realized I was in love with her. I later would realize that I was afraid to allow myself to fall in the beginning. I had suffered much pain due to Kathy's death and the debacle with Jenna. I still do not consider what I had with Jenna a marriage. To me, placing that in the same category with my marriage to Kathy and what I have had with Maggie is an insult to both.

Meanwhile I was working hard and learning the business. Within ninety days I had discovered two things: The search business was not what I had believed it to be. Secondly I realized I had a gift. The bottom line is that I was in the people business. The more I learned about myself, the better I became in my job. TJ had mentioned her idea to franchise the business. Once I had mastered the basics, we began the process. I knew nothing about franchising a business, and neither did she. So I attended a couple of seminars with the International Franchise Association. I found a good franchise attorney, who put together a *prospectus* for us. Then I set out to find potential franchisees. Within two years I had offices in every region of the country. I trained all of them, managed them, and then trained all their associates.

One of the first offices I set up was in the Philadelphia area. I was working there one week, and Maggie came up on Friday. I was to finally meet her dad and all her family. To her surprise and mine, her dad and I connected immediately. In time, we would become very close. I also met her two older sisters and that, too, went well.

I continued to work and build my business. One of the most stressful things people engage in is making career moves. I soon learned that all the psychology I had learned in my own healing was a huge benefit in counseling others. I was able to help them face their fears and emotional upheavals, which always came somewhere in the process. People came to depend on me, including my coworkers. I realized I was helping others, and it felt good. I had not expected any of this but became grateful I had chosen this path. We all reach crossroads in our lives, several of them. The night John confronted me had proved to be a major crossroads for me. It had changed my trajectory completely. I did not realize this at the time. I came to realize we all have freedom of choice and come to crossroads in our lives. From that point, every time I had a major decision to make, I saw it as a crossroads. There have been so many in my life. I learned to allow time to be my ally. Occasionally, the best decision is no decision at all.

During this period, I continued to attend my meetings, at AA and at MARR. More importantly, I continued to practice the principles in all my affairs. Maggie was doing the same thing, and we did this together. We eventually moved in together. We both had reservations about it, especially her. She knew her dad would not approve. We did not lie to him, but neither did we mention it. I am confident he suspected but never asked. There was also the matter of trying to do what was morally correct. Then we realized we were together all the time anyway. It made no sense paying rent on two apartments. So we found a nice two-bedroom apartment in Peachtree Corners. At Christmas Maggie gave me a cat. I grew up with cats and dogs. I mention this because I never felt at home without animals around. I just could not believe how happy I was. Less than two years earlier, I had been in darkness. My life had been destroyed. Then one day I realized that I had not had a desire to drink since I was admitted into MARR. I came to believe in miracles. There was no doubt to anyone that my life was a miracle.

Two months before my second AA anniversary, Maggie and I became engaged. She was Catholic, and I was

Episcopal. The Catholic Church had a problem approving of the marriage because, technically, I was divorced. She had been attending my church with me anyway. One Sunday we were attending mass, and I noticed this priest. He looked so familiar to me. He looked like Father Gary from my church in Greensboro, the same priest who had done the service at Kathy's funeral. I thought no, it can't be. We were at the Cathedral of St. Philip in Buckhead. It was one of the largest Episcopal churches in the county. I had given Maggie her engagement ring during a mass in the small chapel there. After the service that Sunday, I walked back to the area where the offices were. I spotted him and said, "Father Gary?" He turned and saw me. I walked over, and he gave me a big hug, obviously as surprised to see me as I was him. We sat down, and I brought him up to date. He told me how many prayers he had said for me and how worried he had been. He was visibly very happy to see me and the new life I had found. I introduced him to Maggie, and they connected immediately. Later we asked him to perform our wedding ceremony. We were required to go through counseling by the Church. I still recall the assessment of the therapist. He said Maggie was a *realist* and that I was a *dreamer*. At the time I did not agree but would later realize he was on target. It was important that we both understood these characteristics going into the marriage.

When Kathy died someone gave me a book. It was

called *Life after Life* by Dr. Raymond Moody. It was about the thousands of cases of near-death experiences. Patients who were pronounced dead had returned to tell similar stories. I had found this book so comforting. There have since been several books describing the same stories. Then I recalled the stereo coming on and my conversations with Kathy about how she would contact me if there was a way. A few weeks before Maggie and I were to be married, I was in Southern California on business. I had opened an office there. My best friend, David, and his wife, Louise, were living in Huntington Beach. So I stayed over the weekend to visit with them. David and I had met in New York City years before. We had visited many times over the years, so he knew Kathy well. Louise had met her but did not know her as well. So we went to dinner on Saturday night on Balboa Island. It was a place called Magic Island. They boasted of having authentic clairvoyants, mediums, and palm readers. We had dinner and frankly never thought about anything except catching up. We mostly spoke of old times together. After dinner we were ready to leave when Louise said we should have our palms read. I was not interested but went along. We sat at a table with a middle-aged woman. David went first, and we were shocked at how accurate she was on him. Then it was my turn. She asked for my hand and immediately said, "Ah, you have the big 'M.'" I did not know what she meant initially, so she said, "You are getting married." David and Louise knew I was, but we had not discussed it during dinner. This was interesting, but what came next blew me away. She said, "You have been married before." I nodded that I had, and she told me my wife had died a painful death. She then said Kathy was there, standing directly behind me. She then proceeded to describe Kathy perfectly: brown hair, brown eyes, and a beautiful face. I could feel her, and all the hair on my neck was standing up. She then told me that Kathy had a message for me. She said, "I got your letter, and I am so happy for you in your forthcoming marriage." I was white as a sheet. No one there had any way of knowing what was meant by the letter except me. It was the letter I had written to her and read in my group. I cannot describe how this made me feel, but I felt great. The session ended with her telling me that I was very clairvoyant too. I did not give her comment a second thought at the time but would later.

David still lives in California and is still my best friend to this day. We still talk about that evening, which was well over thirty years ago. The bottom line is that I knew Kathy was with me and helping me. Maggie and I believe to this very day she had something to do with us being together.

We were married in the main cathedral at high noon, Saturday, September 9, 1989. It was a beautiful day, not a cloud in the sky. It was a relatively large wedding. During the ceremony, we both experienced something that is hard to explain. We were literally bonded together in holy matrimony. Suddenly there were two bodies but only one spirit. We would later discuss this feeling with each other. Independent of one another, we had had the exact same experience and feeling. This bond has never been broken. We had a beautiful reception at Anthony's in Buckhead. Kathy's brother Rick and his wife, Melanie, were there. At one point Rick came to me and said, "Harry, do you know who Maggie reminds me of?" I said I didn't, and he replied, "Kathy." I was truly taken back and said, "No way." Eventually I knew he was right, but at the time I just could not bear comparing anyone to Kathy. There was only one Kathy, and to compare was like saying I was replacing her with Maggie. I love Maggie to my core, but I have never ceased loving Kathy. Anyway this was a beautiful day in every way. Maggie and I were on top of the world with happiness. The following day we flew to the Cayman Islands for a weeklong honeymoon.

When Maggie and I returned from our honeymoon, we resumed our daily routines. We attended our meetings, and I continued building my business. One evening we went to a movie called *Somewhere in Time*. It was a powerful love story of two people who met, fell madly in love, and then one died. He was reborn and came back to find her still alive, somewhere in time. Maggie and I bought a CD with the soundtrack. One Saturday I was home alone with the music playing. The CD had finished playing, and shortly afterward Maggie came home. She walked in and looked around and said, "Kathy is here!" I felt it too, and the feeling of her presence was so strong we did not second-guess it. It did not spook either of us. We still recall that moment to this very day.

The surprising thing to most people was how Maggie reacted to all of this. She completely accepted that Kathy was part of my life. She told me how she would talk to Kathy sometimes. She thanked her for helping make me into the man I was and promised to take good care of me. When we moved in together, I had the needlepoint Kathy had done for me—which was given to me the Christmas after her death—in a box. Of course it was so special to me, but I did not want to make Maggie uncomfortable. She spotted it and said, "No, this will go on a wall in our home." It was hung and is still on a wall in our home today. I vividly remember Kathy's mom and dad coming for a visit. When her mom saw the needlepoint on the wall, she was taken back. She turned to me and said, "Harry, she allows you to have this?" I said, "Yes, in fact, she insisted." Her mom and dad were so impressed. Her mom told me I was a very lucky man to have found Maggie. They loved her from that day forward.

During one of my brief periods of sobriety when I was still with Jenna, she told me about Silva Mind Control. She said it was based on science, and I would like it. I thought, "Yeah, pseudoscience." She tried to get me to meet with this woman Carolyn, who was the Silva instructor. I declined! Jenna was dumb as a box of hammers, and no way would she know about anything that would interest me. But she would not back off. I finally agreed to talk with Carolyn. I would give her ten minutes. Two and a half hours later, I was still talking with her. I agreed to attend the seminars, which would be held over two weekends, two weeks apart. A man named Jose Silva had been researching mind control for decades. The basic premise was this: We all know that kids are so impressionable. They are sponging up everything, like being programmed. The reason is that kids are walking around in alpha brain wave. As adults we are walking around in beta, or superconsciousness. We are in alpha when we are barely awake, like just before we fall asleep or are just waking up. The reason this all made sense to me was because I had had a lot of formal training involving brain wave, EEG as well as EOG (eye movement) along with EKG and EMG (muscle activity). I was trained on the effects of sedative hypnotics on sleep patterns. I even did a preceptorship at Henry Ford Hospital in Detroit in their sleep lab. By watching the grafts measuring heart, eyes, muscle, and brain wave, we could easily tell whether a person was awake, asleep, dreaming, or in deep sleep. So the Silva method was about using techniques to slow the brain wave down to alpha while awake. When in alpha, which was called going to level, one could even reprogram bad habits, create what we wanted to happen, and do many other things. This was accomplished by using breathing techniques, visualization, and imagination.

Initially it took a while to reach level. Then we were taught a technique called the three-fingers technique. We were programmed, at a deep level, that by placing the thumb, forefinger, and index fingers together, we would automatically be transported to level. The idea was that, if you could visualize something you wished for while at level, it would happen. Naturally we were all skeptical.

The first weekend seminar was held in early December. So it was the Christmas season, and people were shopping. One of the ideas had to do with getting parking places, like at the mall. The following Saturday, I had to run an errand at the mall. I knew it would be packed. So when I got into the car, I decided to give it a try. I used the three-fingers technique, visualized an empty parking space right by the door at the mall. It was about a fifteen- to twenty-minute drive. When I reached the mall and got to the area of the door I had visualized, there was a car just backing out as I drove up. I could not believe it, but then I saw who was driving that car. It was Carolyn! She saw me and just held up her three fingers and smiled. I was blown away. However, this was not the end of the story. The following weekend I was back attending the second half of the seminar, called the basic lecture series. Carolyn asked this lady to describe what had occurred with her at the mall the previous Saturday. She had used the technique to get her parking space, and as she was backing out, she saw Carolyn moving into the space she had just vacated. Then Carolyn tells everyone about me being there as she was backing out. There was no way this was a coincidence, and I never questioned the validity after this. Of course this was just elementary stuff, the tip of the iceberg. I completed the seminar but ended up drunk again. Now I am sober and began thinking about it again. I told Maggie about it, and we both attended the basic lecture series together.

Eventually I would attend the advanced courses with Jose Silva himself. I used this method to build my business. I had so many things occur that stunned me, and things happened that there was no explanation for. One of the side benefits was that it taught me how to meditate. This was crucial to my spiritual evolution and to building a relationship with God. Everyone talks about the power of prayer. I came to understand that prayer is talking to God. Meditation is listening to God. I have used the following analogy many times to make my point. If you telephone someone, ask a question, and then hang up before they can answer, what is the point? God always hears us, and he answers us. *No* is also an answer, as I discovered many times. I can hear God, but I must be quiet and at level. I did have one major issue: I just could not visualize God. I know people who say they see God as this old man with a beard. I tried this, but as my perception of God changed, it was not working for me. God is everywhere, in every living thing. I just could not see him as a man anymore. I do consider myself a Christian and could visualize Jesus.

This completely changed my relationship with the Lord. I began developing a very personal relationship with him. That relationship exists to this day but has improved year after year. Jesus is always with me. I am still working on maintaining my conscious contact with him daily.

Chapter 11

A New Way of Seeing

NEXT, I BECAME interested in the art of *seeing*. I had read a book on quantum physics 101. The idea was that we are all energy, vibrating at a certain level. All living things are energy. In fact, everything we see is energy. A stone is energy, a very dense energy. When we look at someone or something, what do we see? We usually see what we think we will see. What happens when we have misplaced something and begin searching for it? I have found many times that I had been looking directly at it and failed to see it. It had been just under my nose. Why does this happen? It is all about seeing what we think we will see.

Maggie and I attended a show in Atlanta involving all things spiritual. There was a man with a camera taking photos of people. This was not a normal camera but would capture people's auras. Maggie had a light green aura around her, with white mixed in. The green is indicative of someone who is very giving, like a nurse. My aura was mostly white. The man told us this was rare and that it indicated I was a very spiritual person. I was taught to see auras around people, trees, flowers, etc. I learned to do this in minutes. Just soften your gaze and look just beyond whomever you are looking at. Seeing colors took a lot of practice. The point is that all living things are energy.

Maggie Newberry
Colors of orange and green

A thought, any thought, moves energy, and energy changes matter. I have awakened many mornings thinking of someone. Later that day I would receive a phone call from the person, often someone I had not spoken to in ages. This is not just coincidence. A thought is instantaneous. A person could be anywhere in the world, and your thought reaches them. I realized I was awakening to another world around me, one I had been oblivious to my entire life. I came to understand that we are not just our body and certainly not just our brain. We are connected to each other and everything in the world. The Silva method helped me to access so much of this.

CHAPTER 12

Mind Control

TO BRIEFLY EXPLAIN the mind control method, I was told to think of a room where I felt most safe and protected. I chose my bedroom in the home I was born and raised in. Then I was to imagine a secret door that no one could see except me. Next I was to walk through the door and see steps going down to a landing. On the wall above the landing, I was to see a screen. I was to visualize the number one, three times then take another step down and visualize number two three times. I was to imagine the numbers changing colors. Then I was to take another step and visualize the number three, three times. Then I was at level. To go deeper I was to turn and see more steps and begin the same process. When I reached the bottom, I could go anywhere with my mind. I could continue going deeper and deeper and arrive at my lab. In the lab, there are two screens. If I had a problem, a challenge, I would see it vividly in the screen to my left. Once I see it in its entirety,

I break the mirror. In the next screen/mirror, I visualize what I want to have happen. I make it as real as possible. Then I slowly bring myself back up, in a methodical way. I would continue going back daily and repeating this process. My business took off like a rocket. I could use this method to relax my entire body and, while at this level, pray and meditate.

It is so powerful. Nothing improved my personal relationship with the Lord better than this. When I continued with the advanced course with Jose Silva, it got deeper and deeper. One of the things I learned was how to scan people to diagnose a medical issue. For example, one of my classmates would say something like this, "I am thinking of my mother. She is seventy-five years of age and lives in Richmond, Virginia, in a brick home." While at a deep level of my mind, I would go there and scan her from head to toe. I might see a darkness over her heart. I would say it appears she has heart trouble. My classmate would confirm that she did. I would switch places, and I would offer a case with someone I knew. Time after time we were correct. So were the other members in the class. The next step was to send the person suffering white energy for healing, to reduce pain, or general healing. I recall doing this one afternoon around 3:00 p.m. That evening my partner called his family member and asked how she was doing. She said she had felt terrible all day but began feeling much better that afternoon around 3:00 to 4:00 p.m. This, too, happened over and over. I was certainly more than intrigued but knew I was not changing careers. The important thing was that this opened my mind and introduced me to the world around me, one that I had never known existed.

CHAPTER 13

The Search for Truth and Answers

AFTER KATHY AND my family had died, I began asking questions. At some point in life, most of us ask questions such as these: Why am I here? What happens after death? What is the purpose of life? When I read Dr. Moody's book *Life after Life*, it opened me to so many questions. When I got sober, my inquisitiveness went into overdrive. The deeper I investigated my own heart, the more I began understanding. I began reading everything I could find. I was reading two books per week, looking for answers. I began studying other religions and reading the words of spiritual gurus, hoping they could give me the answers I sought. Finally I read about a man who was searching for the same answers as I was. He had lived in the 1800s. He had finally realized that no one could provide answers to his questions. He realized he would have to find them for himself. I did not stop reading, but I, too, came to understand I would have to find my own answers.

Meanwhile Maggie and I were so happy. I had opened several offices, but we were not earning the income we had expected. I discovered that, although doing this work came naturally to me, most just could not do it. All I was doing was training new associates. We realized there was a 95 percent turnover rate. TJ and I would look at each other and say, "What is it? Why can't these people do this?" I had a man in my San Francisco office who was literally a genius. He could make me feel like an idiot, but he could not buy a deal.

Finally TJ came to me and wanted me to buy her out. I owned 50 percent of the franchise operation, but she owned the Atlanta office outright. Initially I was going to do it. Maggie and I went to her dad for the money. She had money in a trust and asked him for some of it. He finally agreed, but I got cold feet. I prayed and meditated about it, and it just did not feel right. I realized I was at a major crossroads. In the past, I knew I would have gone through with it, but this time I trusted my gut. I also knew, if I failed, it would hurt my relationship with her dad. I knew that doing business with family is dangerous. So instead I decided to open my own office. Maggie and I still had the money from her dad, but we returned it. I did need money to start the business, so I went to some men I knew and took venture capital. This meant 20 percent interest per year. I knew it was a risk, but I believed in myself. So I began, and by the end of my first year, I was on fire and had paid back all the venture capital money. Suddenly I was earning more income than ever before. I had also gotten my driver's license back. To this day, I do not know how I managed to travel all over the country and build a nationwide business with no driver's license. I admit I did drive some, to and from work. I was scared to death every time I did it. I still consider it a miracle in my life that I managed to get through this period. So the day I got a Georgia driver's license was then and remains one of the happiest days of my life.

To celebrate, I bought a new car. I got a new BMW 5 Series. I was ecstatic to say the least. Maggie and I had bought a nice little house in Peachtree Corners, not far from our first apartment. This was in our first six months of marriage. Two years after I started my own business, six years after we were married, we bought a new home. It had five bedrooms, five full baths, and a finished basement. The home was just under construction when we found it. When we were first married, we wanted children. We began trying to get her pregnant almost immediately. It never happened. We spent over $50,000 on infertility treatments, but they could never give us a medical reason as to why it was not happening. Maggie was on all these hormones that made her crazy. In the end we gave it up. It felt as if we were questioning God's will. I also felt these drugs were harming Maggie. Although I am not talking a lot about this issue here, I cannot even begin to explain how hurtful this was to us. It still is, but we did have to accept it.

When we moved into the new home, we were so excited. However, within a year it was just a home, and my new BMW just became a car that got me from one place to another. Running that big house was like running a business. We realized that we were happier in our first little home. It reminded me of how I felt during all my success before Kathy died. In retrospect, I think I was doing this to impress others, like my father-in-law. I also wanted to show the people who had put me down because of my alcoholism. This also included myself. I finally realized that I had reverted to my old thinking. I was again seeking happiness from material things outside myself. I had fallen into old thinking. There was nothing wrong with having a nice home and car. It was how I held it all within myself. Once we settled in, I restarted my search. I began reading again. I had also become a gym rat. I had been told I had to take care of myself spiritually, mentally, and physically. Of course I was and am still an alcoholic. For me, anything worth doing is worth overdoing. I had a trainer at the gym and went every day. This would continue for many years.

One of the things I learned in mind control was to watch every word I said. The brain is like the hard drive on a computer. It takes every word literally. For example, a phrase people often use is, "That man is a pain in my ass."

By saying this, you end up with hemorrhoids. Another is, "That burns me up." Then you begin sweating profusely. Although this is all very true, it helped me begin monitoring my words and my thoughts. The Bible says we are made in the image of God. God is the creator, and so are we. We create our own life and reality. By continuing to use the Silva method to build my business, I came to know we are indeed creators. We are responsible for our own lives. This was no longer an opinion, but a fact. A fact I had proven to myself repeatedly. Our brain is a very powerful tool, but it is not who we are. This is another reason we know that maintaining a positive attitude is critical. Never say, "I can't." If you think you cannot, then you cannot. If we are thinking bad or evil thoughts about someone, we indeed do them harm. Thought moves energy, and energy changes matter.

I had discovered how my brain was a great *tool*. I had also learned I could not think my way into happiness. The key was to learn to live more in my heart and follow my intuition, that little voice we all hear occasionally. Gurus and teachers often tell their students to *follow their heart*. Unfortunately in my experience, most people do not. We all allow our heads to overrule our heart. I finally realized that every single time I went against what my heart said and followed my head, I regretted it. To me, my heart is the God within. The answers to all my questions are in there. This is another reason why quiet meditation is so crucial.

If we do not go within, "we go without." Explaining or writing about this topic is not easy. Yet it was the biggest revelation I had found in my life at that point. I also discovered I had to practice this every day. Again just possessing this knowledge was worthless unless I used it.

I began to access where I was, especially spiritually. Spiritual gurus often talk about people going through life deaf, blind, and dumb. I began to comprehend what they meant. I had lived all my life completely unaware of the spirit world around me. I thought I was my intellect. I had known nothing of the energy that flows through all of us and everything around us. I had no idea that we are all connected. I was waking up! When I got into recovery and was given all the tools to live by, initially I thought they were just for alcoholics. The moment I reentered the professional workplace, I began to see how these tools were for everyone. The sad thing was how few people used these tools. Worse yet, they were not aware they existed. Because my work involved a lot of counseling, I began sharing them. People would often ask, "How do you know all this?" I never criticized them. How could I? I had not known many of them myself, even though I was raised in a wonderful family. What I found so amazing was that these principles have been around throughout human history. Everyone should be practicing these simple principles. Parents should be teaching their children to use these tools from birth. After thinking about this many times over the years, it is not surprising to see how so many people are unhappy and full of anger. Perhaps the saddest thing is that it is getting worse. Age has its drawbacks, but one thing it does give us is perspective. I have watched the country I love fall into a continuous state of moral decay. Just in the past twenty years, it has decayed so much. Crime rates and suicides have accelerated beyond belief. Every adult I speak with seems to have this terrible feeling about the future and the direction we are heading in. This is one of the many reasons I decided to write this book.

I had continued going to my AA meetings. When I had had two years of sobriety, my sponsor, Bob, was celebrating five. This is a milestone, and he chose to celebrate it at a large AA clubhouse. He invited his dad, who held a doctorate in theology. He held a high-level position in the Southern Baptist Convention. The meeting was a general discussion, and there were many people there who were still in early sobriety. In meetings like this, you will hear a lot of four-letter words, and this meeting was no exception. As we sat there and the bad language poured out, Bob and I looked at each other. We did not know how his dad would react. We both knew many so-called Christians who would have walked out, but his dad seemed to be listening intently. After the meeting we all went to dinner. After we finished our meal, Bob asked his dad what his impressions of the meeting were. We were dying to know. I will never forget what he told us. After some thought he slowly began to speak. He looked at Bob and said, "Son, what I witnessed there tonight is what churches have been trying to accomplish for centuries." He did not even mention the profanity. He was able to see far beyond that and look at the honesty and devotion to a power greater than ourselves. I began to realize what a true gift I had been given. AA became my church. I have gotten so much more from these meetings than have ever received in any church service.

I continued to search. I was constantly reading. Along the way I read that there are only two emotions: love and fear! Initially I thought, "No, that cannot be right, can it?" Then I began thinking about it. We live in the world of *relativity*. God lives in the world of the *absolute*. Thus we read the "I am that I am" in the Bible. In the celestial world, for everything there is a polar opposite. Examples are hot and cold, up and down, male and female, etc. Everything is energy! For an electrical current, we must have a positive and a negative charge. So with emotions, we have love and fear. Fear can manifest in many ways: anger is fear turned outward, depression is fear turned inward—envy, jealousy, hatred, violence, crime, murder, and greed. Love is joy, happiness, and peace.

We also have been given the power of choice. On any given day, we are either coming from within ourselves from a place of love or fear. Most of us have some of both. Feelings are neither right nor wrong; they just are. The best way to change how I feel is to first change my thinking, using the tools and principles I have been taught. If I find myself in fear, I automatically ask myself, What I am afraid of? If it is something I can do nothing about, then I must accept it. I use a prayer called the Serenity Prayer daily. "God, grant me the serenity to accept the things I cannot change, the courage to change the things I can, and the wisdom to know the difference." I realize this sounds too simple, but it has worked for me for decades. It has kept me out of deep intellectual analysis. This basic concept provided the foundation I needed to live a happy life, which was my goal. I have learned that simple practices are the most effective. I use what has been called the KISS principle. Keep it simple, stupid! I have never known anyone too stupid to use these tools, but I have known people too smart. I admit that in the beginning I might have been too smart for my own good. I would be told about these tools, and it went in one ear and out the other. I would think, "Yeah, I got it," but did not use any of them in my daily life.

Chapter 14

Peru Journey

As the years passed, I had practiced these principals daily. They became a part of me, second nature. Maggie and I were so happy, and my business was thriving. We took vacations all over this country and out of it. We went to London and to Paris. I continued to work out in the gym and was in excellent physical condition. Although I was very happy, I was still hungry for truth and answers about life. I sought spiritual enlightenment continuously. I had read so many books and studied various religious teachings but had not found what I was looking for. I had been on this quest since the death of Kathy and my family. At some point, I realized I would have to find my own answers. Then, I read a book called *The Celestine Prophecy*, by Jim Redfield. It was defined as a fictional parable, with the setting in Peru. After reading it, I could not get it out of my head. It was a wonderful story, but I was more intrigued by Peru. This intrigue continued for many weeks. Finally,

I realized I needed to go there. I discussed it with Maggie and with my sponsor, Bob. Both asked me why, and I had no answer. I tried to convince them to go with me, but they declined. One thing I had learned was to listen to my heart, to follow it. I finally realized this was my journey. Maggie agreed but was concerned. I began planning.

Harry at Machu Picchu

I had seen a story on the Discovery Channel about this amateur archeologist from Chicago. He had made a discovery at Machu Picchu, and another one in the area. I contacted him, and we began a friendship. He connected me with several people, in Lima and in Cusco, Peru. Once I had everything in place, I booked a flight and took off alone. I had no idea what to expect nor even what I was looking for. I landed in Lima very early in the morning. I had heard the airport could be a dangerous place to spend time. I had two people pick me up and drive me to an apartment. My flight to Cusco was around 11:00 a.m. So, when the time grew near, they drove me back to the airport and I boarded the flight. Cusco sits at 11,300 feet above sea level. Flights can only go in there midday due to the updraft coming from the Amazon jungle. When I landed, Zoilo Vargara, a professor at the university, met me. He drove me directly to my hotel and had me drink a cup of coca tea and go to bed. This was to give my body time to acclimate to the altitude. It takes a couple of weeks to fully acclimate, to build enough red blood cells to carry more oxygen into our brain and body. Later that day Zoilo and his assistant, Violetta, returned and took me to dinner.

Tourism is a huge business there. To be a guide required a degree, and this is what Zoilo taught. To obtain a degree required a lot of knowledge in many areas—history, archeology, anthropology—and a deep knowledge of every ruin, which are many. They also need a great understanding of spirituality and mysticism. I spent two weeks there. The first week was very hard on me physically. I had no energy, and even walking was difficult. I had not expected this. The phrase I came to despise was, "And now we go up." From Cusco, everywhere we went was up, higher altitude. We did a lot of sightseeing my first week. One of these places was Sacsayhuamán, which sits above Cusco. It is one of the most incredible creations known to man. It was constructed as a fortress to protect Cusco, which was the capital of the ancient Incan empire. Some of the stones are the size of buses and cars. The amazing thing is that all the stones are different sizes but are fitted together so tightly you cannot slide a thin sheet of paper, or even a hair, between them. I saw many similar-type constructions all over the country. Even today, with modern engineering and machines, no one has been able to duplicate this level of construction.

Winter solstice Celebration in Cusco 1998

We then left for Machu Picchu. It is a four-hour train ride thru the Urubamba River valley. I was amazed at the things I saw. It was like going back in time over fifty years. The Indians, the Quechua, live just as they did before the Spanish invaded. Both Zoilo and Violetta told me these people would be afraid of me. All the people were very short in stature, with a big chest and short legs. Over many generations they had been genetically engineered for these mountains. I am six feet three and 210 pounds and have bright-blue eyes. When we encountered the Quechua, they were all amazed to look at me. However, these people did not back off from me as I had been told. Instead, they walked right up to me and began talking. Zoilo translated, as he spoke Quechua. They treated me as a friend, almost like they knew me. Zoilo and Violetta were blown away. They said they had never seen this. They continued talking about it, even after we returned to Cusco. I eventually learned the reason for this. They had been taught to see a person's aura. This was just a part of who they are. Mine is white, denoting a spiritual person, so they being spiritual people immediately trusted me. I can see auras too. It is very easy, but seeing colors is another matter. I have seen colors around a few people, but I am not proficient at it.

When we arrived at the train station below Machu Picchu, we began climbing the mountain. I did much better there because the altitude is only around eight thousand feet. Still, it almost killed me. I was still living in Atlanta at this time, which is only about one thousand feet above sea level. That evening I stayed at the small hotel, just outside the entrance of the citadel. Zoilo knew the security people there, so after it was closed to the public, we were allowed to enter. It was as if I had it all to myself. Of course, I had no idea what I was looking at, so Zoilo walked with me and explained the meaning of many things.

I was getting tired and found a large grassy area below the structure where he said the Inca leaders would stand and address the people. I decided to lie down to rest. Zoilo left me alone. I then decided to meditate and took myself to a very deep level. I had gone down so fast, like a stone falling to the bottom. I might have fallen asleep. Anyway, I began having very vivid images, seeing all these people. They wore very bright colors and headdress. I had seen some of this in Cusco. As the Quechua still dressed just as they had in ancient times, it felt as if I was watching a movie. Then something happened that I have never been able to reconcile. The Quechua began to see me, to interact with me. I later decided that I had just fallen asleep and was dreaming. Still, I had never had an experience like that and haven't had one like it since. What haunted me for years was what they said to me. I am not going to go into it here, but suffice it to say, it served to expand my consciousness. To me, it really does not matter whether it was real or not. It did propel me to continue my quest.

The next day we climbed Huayna Picchu. It is almost

straight up and overlooks Machu Picchu. I found myself hanging by a rope with a thousand-feet drop straight down into a river. I made it to the top, but coming down was equally as treacherous as the climb up. I was beyond exhausted. Later that day we boarded the train to return to Cusco. The engine was pushing on the return, versus pulling, so I was seated on the very front. The view was incredible. I was sitting next to a German woman, and we enjoyed the trip together. Then the train stopped at a station and she got off. When she returned, she had cheese and crackers. I was famished since I had had nothing to eat since early that morning. We had just made the train when we came off the mountain. So when the lady offered me some of the food, I gladly accepted. When we arrived back in Cusco, I was dropped off at my hotel and left on my own for dinner. I was not feeling well but attributed it to being exhausted. I went out to eat but could not finish my meal, which was odd, considering the fact I had eaten very little that day. So I went to bed. I was suddenly awake and running for the bathroom. I was violently ill. This continued all night, back and forth to the bathroom. The next morning Zoilo and Violetta arrived to take me on a trip they had planned. I could not go. I was so weak and still sick.

Maggie and I had planned to talk by phone that evening. I knew she would be visiting her dad in Philadelphia. That night I was excited to call her. I missed her terribly. When she answered the phone, the first words out of her mouth were, "You are sick, aren't you?" I said, "How did you know that?" She proceeded to tell me a story. That morning she had a girlfriend drive her to the Atlanta airport. They were only a couple miles from our home when she told her friend to pull over quickly. Maggie exited the vehicle and began throwing up. When she got back in the car, her friend, who was alarmed, said, "What is going on?" Maggie replied, "Harry is sick. I can feel it." I was amazed when she told me, but not surprised. I had told you earlier about when we were married. We were literally bonded in holy matrimony. We feel what the other feels. For example, if I am out during the day and return home, I know whether she is feeling bad the instant I walk in the door. We never like being apart physically. However, when we are separated, we are always together. We can feel the presence of each other, due to the bond. Today with cell phones, we are always connected. I recently took a long weekend to visit our nephew and his family. We texted at least four or five times a day and talked live at least once. This story is about my inner journey, but Maggie is always with me, always.

Before I left Cusco, I was invited to lecture at the public university there. The topic was on metaphysics and spirituality. I think I did five lectures to different groups of students. They made me an honorary professor and presented me with a handmade plaque, which was done on a special type of tree bark. It hangs in my office to this day. I was very honored. The day before my departure, I took a group of students, around twenty-five, to the temple of the moon at Sacsayhuamán, and taught them prayer and meditation techniques. They loved it.

During my long flight home, I reflected on everything that happened. I had gone there with no expectations. I had followed my heart. There was no doubt in my mind this was meant to be. I experienced things I still cannot explain. I only shared these things with Maggie but otherwise kept them to myself. Many people from all over the world have gone there, but my guess is there are few who were asked to lecture at the university. All I knew for sure was that I felt great and had a peace I had not known before. When I returned, everyone noticed it, including those who knew nothing of my trip. The only thing I was certain of was that, first, I felt great and, secondly, I knew I would return there.

CHAPTER 15

The Shamanic Path Begins

WHEN I RETURNED, I continued with all my routines. I worked, went to the gym, went to AA meetings, and read. I had a friend who owned a book store in Duluth. I asked him to find books on Peru for me. When I went back, he had four books. I bought all of them. Two of the books were by the same author, Dr. Alberto Villoldo, a PhD in psychology. I read both his books in a week. I was blown away at the story he told. While working on his thesis in the early 1970s, he was studying the spiritual practices of the native peoples of the world. He discovered that much of this knowledge within North American natives had been lost. When the whites came in, their lives and practices had been decimated. This had not occurred, not to the same degree, in South America.

He began investigating the Quechua people in Peru.

Like me, he had gone to Cusco, the ancient capital of the Inca Empire. While there, he met a sociology professor at the university. The same one with whom I had done the lectures. This man was a wealth of knowledge but told him to understand that he would have to go within himself. He told him that to get where he needed to be quickly, he could go into the Amazon jungle and meet with this jungle shaman. There he could participate in an *ayahuasca* ceremony. *Ayahuasca* is a vine that grows in the jungle and is the most powerful psychic substance known to man. Many call it the "rope of death." It is brewed in a big pot, along with some other leaves, such as the datura leaf, which is very toxic. He had told Alberto he needed to be purified. He was also told he had to be rid of his fear of death to be free. This substance would take him to death and beyond. I had deduced that Alberto and I were about the same age. All this had occurred in the very early 1970s. I had experimented a bit with LSD back then, but this made LSD look like aspirin.

I thought this man must have been out of his mind. Yet I could not put down the book. He goes into the jungle and finds this man. It is just the two of them, in the middle of nowhere. He is handed a cup of the substance and drinks it. Within a short while, he is out in the jungle evacuating everything in his body. It is coming out of every orifice. This is the purification. Afterward, his journey begins. He travels through the dark curtain and enters the next world. Once we realize there is no death, only that of our body, we are no longer afraid of it. This gives us a freedom like we have never known. While reading this I began feeling this horrible fear. I just could not imagine doing something like that.

The following day Alberto had returned to Cusco. He went directly back and met with the professor. He began to sense something very different about this man. He was told about a myth. When the Spanish conquistadors arrived, the world of the so-called Inca was turned upside down. The spiritual leaders, known as the Q'ero, had seen in visions their arrival. They knew they were coming, and there was nothing they could do to stop it. So they escaped and took their families high into the mountains and had remained there for over five hundred years. Even among the Quechua people, this was just a myth. This professor told Alberto it was no myth; it was true. He became Alberto's teacher.

The second book describes how he trained Alberto, who finally learned that this professor was actually one of the Q'ero. The story was that they would return when the time was right, when the world would be turned right side up again. Their knowledge had remained pure and had never changed. This meant that Alberto was being taught firsthand. He was taught their language and eventually taken to a couple of their villages. They had lived at altitudes above sixteen thousand feet. They farmed and raised llamas. They had lived entirely isolated. They had never seen a car, a radio, a phone, nor anything in the world we live in.

I began making plans to return to Cusco. This time I took a friend of David, from California, and his brother. I connected them with Zoilo for their tour guide and left on my own. I had contacted Alberto's office and learned he was in Peru. It was their winter solstice, a powerful time there. Many ceremonies were held. I found Alberto in Pisac. I was a little anxious about meeting him but was also very excited. We sat down and talked most of the afternoon. I shared with him my journey to that point. He immediately picked up on me and said, "You are on a genuine quest for truth." He invited me to come train with him. He told me about the medicine wheel training—a two-year program where we would first visit the south, receive the teachings, and return home, where we would practice what we were taught for six months. Then we would return for the west, then the north, and finally the east. After the conversation I left and did not see him again for a few months. I attended the ceremonies while there, and they were beautiful.

When I got home, I called his office. Alberto had asked me to call and have some materials sent, including some videotapes. In 1994, the Q'ero had come off the mountain. Alberto had filmed it. There, they delivered their prophecies. They had never seen a globe of the world.

They immediately pointed to the Middle East and said this is a place of great conflict and has been for centuries. Then, they pointed to the United States and said this is a country in conflict with itself. Shortly after this Timothy McVeigh bombed the Alfred P. Murrah Federal Building in Oklahoma City. This was also my first glimpse of them and the colors they wore. They were identical to the ones I had seen in my visions when on Machu Picchu.

A couple months later, I would attend my first training seminar. It was held at a retreat center north of Santa Barbara, California. There was only about nine or ten of us. Some were psychologists, psychiatrists, and mental health professionals. At this point, you could not just sign up. Alberto interviewed and approved of each participant. I remember him telling us two things before we started. First, we would receive many priority and secret teachings and were told never to disclose them. Secondly, he explained that this is not an intellectual path but an experiential one. He explained that the things we would learn were to be incorporated into our daily living. This made sense to me because of all the tools I had been given in my recovery program. They were worthless unless they became me and how I lived every day.

This first set of teachings was the south direction of the medicine wheel. Life is not a straight line but like a wheel. We are born, we live, and we die. All living things go through this circle. The archetype of the south is *sachamama*, the great serpent. A serpent sheds its skin. We go to the south to shed the skin of our past. I thought this is like doing a fourth and fifth step in AA. We were to choose three traumas we had endured and transfer the energy into three stones. The stones would go into our mesa, or medicine bag, and become our power. At the end of this first seminar, we were given assignments to work on over the next six months. Because of all the work I had done for my recovery, I knew I had already completed much of this.

There was one practice of the assignments I had not focused on. This was the practice of nonjudgment. I had never considered myself to be a judgmental person. I quickly learned the fallacy of that belief. Over the following six months, I came to realize I judged everyone and everything. It is very difficult to avoid much of this. We live in a world of relativity. Everything is relative to someone or something else. Then I remembered what I had been taught about only comparing myself to myself. If I looked at where I came from and where I had gotten to in life, I felt great about myself. When I compared myself to others who seemed to have accomplished much more, I felt a failure. This served no one, especially not me. However, it was not just about judging others. It was about judging everything as good or bad, every situation, every crisis.

How do we know if something is good or bad in the moment? For example, when I finally realized I was an alcoholic, I concluded that was the worst thing that could have happened to me. Today, and even back at that time, I know that it is one of the best things that could have happened. I do not mean the alcoholism in and of itself, but the path it sent me down. I know there was no way I would have ever gotten on the spiritual path, found the relationship I have with God, had that not occurred. I would have probably become a wealthy man living a very shallow life. I would have never awakened to the energetic and spiritual world around me. I would have carried the same old baggage for the rest of my life. My ultimate goal of "being happy" would have never been realized. I would have only known temporary happiness but obtaining material possessions outside myself.

When I returned for the west training, Alberto asked me how I did. I told him not well at all. I explained how I had discovered how judgmental I had been all my life. He pointed out that none of us are perfect, but the good news was that I was now aware. He said this is a journey and the practice of nonjudgment is just that, practice, not perfection. I have come a long way, but I am still practicing today.

The archetype of the west is the black jaguar. In Quechua, he is called "otorongo." Metaphorically, we ride on its back across the rainbow bridge to death and beyond. I had tried understanding death for years at this point. I had come to believe in life after life. I knew Kathy had remained a part of my life. Too many things had happened for me to just write it off as coincidence. We went through several exercises that were so powerful. In the end it was clear to me what he was insinuating. If I truly wanted to know there was no death, I would have to go there via an *ayahuasca* journey in the Amazon jungle. At the time, I had no intentions of doing that.

Six months later I was in the mountains of Utah doing the north direction. The archetype of the north is the hummingbird, or *see-wac-kenta*. This is where we go to access the knowledge of our ancestors, the old ones. I was to become a shaman of the north. I was fascinated by the techniques I was taught. Other than with Kathy, I was never able to communicate with my mom and dad, nor my brother.

There had been another death in my immediate family. Marty, my nephew, who was my brother's son, had died in 1994 of pancreatic cancer. He and I were raised like brothers. He was the same age as Maggie, four years younger than me. I was sober by that time. His wife had called me and said the doctors were giving him only thirty days to live. He had not begun to get his affairs in order. So I drove up and met with his doctors. They confirmed what Connie, his wife, had told me.

I remember the day I went to talk with him so vividly. It was the most difficult thing I have ever done. I had seen him a couple weeks earlier, and he still looked the same, healthy. I told him I had spoken with his doctors, and it was terrible news. "You have maybe thirty days to live." The silence was deafening. When he finally spoke, he said, "Oh my God, who is going to teach Kenny, take him fishing, etc.?" Kenny was his little boy of seven years of age. His daughter was a senior in high school. I promised him I would take care of them. He had built a very successful business with a partner. I helped him get his affairs in order. Sure enough, he died within thirty days. I did take care of Kenny, and to this day he is the closest thing I have to a son. His daughter lives in New York City and seems to want nothing to do with me. God knows I have tried many times. My brother also had a daughter, Rhonda. She died of a cerebral aneurism at age five. Her hair was almost white. She indeed looked like an angel. I have been able to communicate with her several times. Years later, I had some contact with Marty. I have always felt close to all of them. I know they are around me.

You might ask me how I know this. In the beginning it was just a feeling. When I was taught the techniques of the north, I discovered they were there, not all the time but often. I can just call to them and feel their presence immediately. Another huge lesson I learned when I communicated with the old ones was this: there are universal truths that never change. Every generation of spiritually oriented people has discovered these same truths, over and over. An internationally known spiritual guru of the twentieth century had stopped talking in 1925. His name was Meher

Baba. The reason he gave was that it had all been said. There was no point in giving more lessons to people. The answers and all the truth were already here. At the time I was doing my training of the north, I had not known of Meher Baba but was receiving the same messages. The teachings and truths that really matter have been around since the beginning of mankind's history. Yet there are very few people in our culture today that can tell you what they are.

When I look around, turn on the news, watch a movie, or talk with people, I am a witness to the fact that people are not happy. They are so full of anger, which is fear. How many people think politicians can fix everything wrong in this country? I think, "My goodness, do you honestly believe politicians can fix anything, can take away your anger, make you happy?" Why is it that we cannot seem to grasp the simple principal that "you must go within, or you go without." Look into your own heart. Spiritual gurus have been saying this for millennium.

I had learned that no human being, no amount of money, no nice car, nor big house could ever make me happy. There is nothing wrong with having nice things, but to use them to be happy is a waste of time. At best, these things provide temporary happiness. I have seen many individuals who were obviously miserable in their own skin. They meet someone, fall in love, and marry. Six months or perhaps a year or two later, they are divorced. A good marriage is wonderful, your biggest asset. However, if you are not already happy inside your own skin, the marriage will never work. The north training hit home for me. It brought everything I had learned, all the knowledge I had acquired full circle. Life really is not complicated. We create the complications for ourselves. The KISS principal had struck again and in a big way.

Six months later, I returned for the final training, the east direction of the medicine wheel. The archetype of the east is the condor, *hatun kuntur*. Here, having completed all the work of the first three directions, we are able to fly. Our spirits have been released from our bodies, and we can soar with the eagles. The basic meaning to me was freedom. I had been freed from the bondage of self, and my spirit was free to live, to fully appreciate the beauties of life. In all living things I found beauty. I looked at trees differently. Animals and all living things were part of God's creation. I found a deeper meaning to my marriage to Maggie. We were truly one spirit, and we both felt it. I began looking at other people differently. Suddenly, I could see pieces of myself in others. For example, I would attend AA meetings and I could tell you at what point people were in recovery just by listening to what they said. Before, I found myself annoyed when I heard people who had just gotten out of a treatment center "talking the talk." Now, I saw myself back when I had been discharged.

We are all connected as brothers and sisters. I had heard this all my life but now began to see the truth and reality of it. I began to understand that every spiritual teacher had taught the same things. Whether you are a Christian or not, no one can argue that the teachings of Jesus have withstood the test of time. He taught love, forgiveness, and nonjudgment of others. I had come to know that love is the polar opposite of fear, and I wanted to come from within myself from a place of love. I had also learned the hard way the power of forgiveness. Left to my own devices, I would have never forgiven Jenna. When I had, I felt the weight of the world lifted from me. Theologians often argue scripture within the New Testament, but no one can argue what Jesus taught about nonjudgment: "Let he who is without sin cast the first stone." Try finding any ambiguity in that.

One of my pet peeves is when I see so much judgment in churches and by their members. I have witnessed them kick people out for a sin, often the people who need to be there the most. To me, this is the exact opposite of what Jesus taught. We have all heard horror stories of well-intentioned people falling into the grasp of cults, of one man professing to be the second coming, or even God. We had David Koresh, Jim Jones, and Warren Jeffs of the FLDS. The FLDS, or the Fundamentalist Church of Jesus Christ of Latter-Day Saints of the Mormon Church, believed in polygamy, plural marriages. They had a prophet who claimed to be the direct vice of God. What made this story so intriguing was that these people had been born into this and were taught this from birth. Initially, the prophet was an old man. He was marrying young girls that were eighteen or nineteen years old and having sex with them. He was supposed to never die but did, and his son, Warren Jeffs, took over. All marriages were arranged by the prophet. Then, he began forcing young girls, fourteen years old, to marry. In the end it became about money, sex, and brainwashing. They followed Warren Jeffs right off the cliff. He is now in prison. The moral of the story is to never follow a man, or any person. Follow your own heart and the teachings.

At the conclusion of the training of the east, I was given the rights of passage in ceremony, just as I had for the first three directions. For each direction, we transferred all the energy into three stones. So we now had twelve stones in our mesa. Now, a final stone, the lineage stone, would be added. This stone carried the actual bloodline from the Q'ero and Alberto. I was now considered a level-four Andean priest, which meant I carried a full mesa, or medicine bag.

In spring of 2000, we had decided to move to Arizona. I had always wanted to live in the west. So Maggie stayed in Atlanta, until our home could be sold. I moved my business and drove out with my two parrots. Having grown up on a farm, I had always loved animals. They were my playmates. I had dogs and cats throughout my life. However, like the people I loved, they kept dying. My sponsor, Bob, told me the parrots would outlive me. I have a blue and gold macaw and a Moluccan cockatoo, a boy and a girl, respectively. I still have them, and they are my babies. So we drove out together. I had rented an office in Carefree, just north of Scottsdale, and a little bungalow to live in. I loved the desert.

On Saturday mornings I would awaken early and drive to Sedona. There are at least four major vortices there. This is where the energy between this world and the next is thin. One of them is at Cathedral Rock. It is a long and hard climb to reach the top, but I would be up there by 9:00 a.m. every Saturday morning meditating. There was never anyone else up there during this time. I cannot begin to describe how powerful these meditations were for me. A few years later, Sedona became so commercial that this was no longer possible. At the end of the summer, our home sold. I flew back and drove Maggie, our two labs, and our cat across the country. The dogs did great, but our cat cried from Atlanta to Oklahoma. The next day he had laryngitis so bad he could not say anything. We were having a home built, so initially we were all living in my little one-bedroom bungalow. A few weeks later, our home was ready and we were grateful.

I continued training with Alberto. I learned many healing techniques, soul retrieval, and extractions. The extractions were like exorcisms. We would extract entities from people. I was involved in performing one on a woman, and it got on me. I did not realize it until I came home. Maggie saw it too as it went up my arm. This scared me and, although it never got inside me, it was crawling all over me. Fortunately, I knew a technique to remove it. I never did another one after that. I did learn just how real they were.

I also became a teacher for the medicine wheel. I performed healing techniques on many people. Then the word got around that I was this very powerful shaman. This was especially true among the other teachers and shaman. Alberto told me I had achieved mastery. Well, I did not buy it. I had no way to carry this. I would think, "What difference does it make even if it is true?" I had to admit I was getting a lot of positive feedback. I recall working on this woman in Phoenix. She was a good friend of a friend. She had been in therapy for five years and did not feel she was improving. She asked for my help. I did work on her. I checked her chakras, and one was completely blocked. Her energy was not flowing through her at all. Again, I cannot disclose the proprietary techniques I used, but she told me of a trauma she had endured. I used my medicine bag, and she chose a stone, which gave me information needed to clear the blockage. Basically, the bad energy was extracted into the stone, which increased the power of my mesa. I realigned and cleaned all her chakras, and she left. Two days later she called me. She was on top of the world with joy. She said, "Harry, in one two-hour session, you accomplished a hundred times more for me than five years of therapy." She said this was the first time she had felt normal, like her old self, since before the trauma. All I did was direct and wield the energy. I saw myself as an instrument of God. I never took any credit for any of the benefits credited to me. I still do not.

I have had several people ask me why a man of God would travel the shamanic path. This is an honest question but based in a lack of knowledge. We fear what we do not understand. God had literally saved me from total disaster. There was no way possible that I would ever turn my back on him. The practice of shamanism is largely about the use of energy. Sadly, there are evil people in this world. The same energy I used for good, there are those who would use it for evil. The difference has to do with "intent." My intent was always pure, as it was with those around me. This was drilled into all our teachings.

Electricity can light our homes and cook our food, but it can also be used to burn your house down and to murder people. During my years on this path, God was always with me, and if my practices helped people, it was God, using me as his instrument. I never knew a single person along this journey that did not work with God. In fact, when I later entered the Amazon jungle, I met two shaman who were devout Christians. If at any point I would have detected anything remotely close to evil, I would have vanished immediately. In the end, the things I learned on this path not only expanded my consciousness but led me to become a devout Christian. Today, I have a personal relationship with Jesus Christ. He is with me every second of every day. In fact, the true reason I entered the shamanic path was very simple: I was seeking spiritual enlightenment. For me, it was a means to an end, and, believe me, it served its purpose.

Chapter 16

Meeting the Q'ero

A COUPLE YEARS later, we were going to Peru together. Back when I began traveling there, I had hired a tutor to teach me Spanish. I never became fluent but could get what I needed. So when we arrived in Cusco, several of the people went with me. Plus I knew my way around, and Alberto asked for my help. Once everyone had adjusted to the altitude a little more, we had the first big night. We met with the Q'ero. It began with a big fire ceremony. I know this may sound crazy, but all of us could feel spirits around us when they called for the old ones, the gray-haired ones, to come. I have attended many fire ceremonies but none like this one. It was so powerful that every one of us was blown away. These people had come down from the mountain to meet with us. When I looked into their eyes, what I saw was indescribable. I would have given a million dollars for what I saw there. It was pure love and total peace. There were only twelve of us, and none of us ever wanted to leave.

These people, the Q'ero, were arguably the poorest people on earth, but they had everything I had ever wanted.

The next afternoon, we met with them again. We all had many questions. I had brought my old friend Zoilo to translate. The eldest and most respected among them was Don Manuel. He was ninety-four at that time. One of my friends, a psychologist, asked him an esoteric question. I cannot even recall his question, but it does not matter. They were farmers and llama herders, so they spoke using metaphors accordingly. I will never forget Don Manuel's answer. He said, regarding knowledge, "If you cannot grow corn with it, then it is worthless to you."

At the time, I do not think I could fully appreciate the opportunity I had been given. However, I have never forgotten a minute of it. I heard them talk about the spiritual path they walked, the principles they adhered to rigorously. Here was a small group of people who had lived in total isolation for many generations, for well over five hundred years. Still at the end of the day, they spoke of the exact same truths, the same tools, and the same practices that every spiritual guru in human history has taught. I have many times thought of Don Manuel's comment about *if you cannot grow corn with it*. This harkened back to the KISS principle. Keep it simple, stupid!

I asked myself how many times I had overanalyzed and overthought things. I had read mountains of books full of interesting theories and ideas, but they were worthless in helping me to find happiness in life. Anyway, I loved spending time with them, and they seemed to be drawn to me like a magnet. They would tease me and call me *hatun kuntur*. This was in reference to my height. Still I knew that was not it because Alberto, whom they knew well, was the same height as me. Each tribe of the Quechua used a different design on their knitting. I bought a new mesa cloth from the Q'ero and a new poncho. I still have and cherish them to this day. I recall wearing the poncho walking through Cusco. Every Indian I came across immediately recognized the design and treated me with reverence.

Quero people who lived in mountains for over 500 years

The Quero

Chapter 17

First Trip into the Amazon

AFTER A FEW days in Cusco, we boarded a small prop plane for the Amazon. We landed on a small runway and then got on a boat to travel downriver. We finally arrived at this small grass-hut village. So much of the Amazon has been destroyed, but this area remained pristine. The jungle was *alive*. When we left the river and walked into the jungle, the canopy was so thick, we could not see the sky. Walking alone in there is very dangerous. Many people have disappeared, never to be seen again. I was amazed at the wildlife, many species of birds. There were macaws, Amazons, monkeys, and scavengers. I saw an entire ecosystem in a small area.

One day we went by boat further downriver to a place called Monkey Island. I had seen it on the Discovery Channel. There must have been hundreds of monkeys of many species. They were everywhere, swinging through the trees and running on the jungle floor, and would come up to us. It was amazing to me. The next night there was to be an *ayahuasca* ceremony. I had given it a lot of thought but chose not to participate. Instead I worked with two jungle shamans. To this day I do not know how they did it, but I was placed in a trance. I know I did not ingest anything. I was outside the confines of space and time. All of my life, I have had a huge sense of humor. At times, a very sick sense of humor. I began to see and communicate with these funny little demons. I sensed no danger nor any threat from them. They were very ugly, and I told them they were. They just laughed and laughed. In the end, I told them to leave and never return. They did! Since then I still have my sense of humor, but the sick sense of humor has never appeared in me again.

The next thing that began happening with me is I began taking on the persona of a jaguar, a black jaguar. There were other people who witnessed this. I could feel my face and mouth morph, and they told me I looked like a big cat that was ready to pounce. I was aware of myself during this time and recall feeling I could do anything. I had no fear whatsoever. I have no idea how long this lasted, but it had to be several hours.

When I awakened the next morning, people told me they could still see the cat in my face. None of what had occurred made any sense to me. I kept wondering if someone had given me a dose of something without my knowledge. I went to Alberto for answers. He had already heard about it. I just wanted to know what this meant, what it was all about. He said the jaguar is at the top of the food chain, and the spirits were showing me who I was. I still did not understand. He said this meant I was a very powerful medicine man, or shaman. There it was again. I did trust Alberto but decided he must have misunderstood me or had judged me incorrectly. I wanted to speak with the two shamans from the night before, but I did not speak to any Quechua.

I finally got a man who was one of our guides from Cusco. His English was fair, so I attempted to explain what I wanted. One of the shaman was a devout Christian. He said I would become a prophet and a messenger, that I had a special gift and could wield tremendous energy. I admit that I have always had a big ego, which I have fought to overcome for years. Normally this would have all gone to my head. Hey, look at me. I can tell you there was no such effect. Instead it spooked the heck out of me. There is one thing I wish for anyone reading this to understand: this *is not* a story about shamanism. This was simply a path I went down seeking spiritual enlightenment. I wanted to know myself for many reasons. But I had already learned, even then, that the better I knew myself, the closer it brought me to God. I was seeking a clear conscience.

Harry in the Amazon Jungle

Harry's Hut in Amazon

Chapter 18

Risk versus Reward

I RETURNED HOME to Arizona. As always I shared everything with Maggie. We both realized that there were those who wanted me to walk away from the life I had and become a full-time shaman. I already knew that was never going to happen. Maggie knew it too. Yet I also knew I was not finished with it. I felt deep within that I still had more to learn. Before we moved from Atlanta, I had met a group of people who were on this path. Most of them were professional people. One of them was an OB/GYN. He held full-moon fire ceremonies every month behind his home in Lawrenceville. I had attended several of these, and he and I had become friends.

As the full moon was approaching, he called me to make sure I was coming. He said he had someone he wanted me to meet. Her name was Eleanor. She held two PhDs and was a professor at Emory University. He was right! We connected immediately. She was several years older than me and was a Native American. Her husband of many years was from the same part of the country as I was, Appalachia. She was also a master shaman and healer. In addition, she had a mission in the northern Amazon of Peru, near Iquitos. She and I connected at a deep, spiritual level. Following that first meeting, we agreed to meet for lunch one day. We sat down at noon, and the next thing we knew it was 4:30 p.m. The same sort of thing happened on many phone calls. We both felt like we had known one another forever, not only in this life but in previous lives.

I had lost touch with her when we moved to Phoenix but now felt compelled to reach out to her. I shared with her the story of my trip to the Amazon. I told her they were holding *ayahuasca* ceremonies but that I had declined. It just did not feel right to me. I seemed to be, for want of a better word, *commercial*. I also shared the story of what had occurred while working with the two shamans. Unsurprising to me, she understood and did explain it was not drug induced. She did tell me she had seen the power in me the first night we met. I explained what my intentions had always been and that I had no desire to live that life. She then asked me a big question: Why would you think you would need to give up anything and go down that path? I explained that I had witnessed how Alberto lived and most of the others I had been involved with. She looked at me and said, "Harry, look at me and Gary (the man who introduced us). We live normal lives." She taught at the university; he practiced medicine. She then explained that for most who have stepped onto this path, it is about going through life awake and self-aware instead of going through it asleep, unaware of everything around us. There are many ways to help others. She knew what I did for a living and said, "Harry, you have been helping people by coaching them, by providing counsel." She also suggested I should write. Alberto had told me the same thing. I ignored this for many years, until now.

Another year passed. I was still searching for answers and for truth. I just felt something was missing. I began thinking about what a journey with *ayahuasca* might offer me. I knew this was a huge decision and that one must be prepared, physically, mentally, and spiritually. I also knew a must was purity of *intent*. I did believe there was life after life and had certainly had a great amount of evidence to this effect. I was also looking for the real key to life and happiness. I called Eleanor to discuss it. Her reply was, "I was wondering when I would receive this call. It's about time." She knew I was still apprehensive to say the least. She was teasing me to lighten my mood. We then discussed how this would happen. She knew a jungle shaman who was pure, the real thing. His name was Don Francisco.

Most of the shaman had lost their power as they lost their ethics. An income of $1,000 a year there was huge. When people from the US and western European countries had gone there and paid them thousands of dollars, they became full of greed. They had also lost respect for those throwing all this money around. When we compromise our ethics and values, it destroys our soul. We lose our connection with God and the spirit world. I realized why I had felt uneasy on my previous trip into the jungle, that it felt *commercial*. I then understood my feelings had foundation.

Eleanor was scheduled to fly back down to her mission in a month. So I had time to prepare myself. I had to go on a nonfat diet, no meat, especially no red meat. I ate mostly a vegetarian diet during this period. I was nervous but also excited. I had time to reflect on the path I had stepped onto years earlier. I recalled reading Alberto's first book about his trip into the jungle alone to do the *ayahuasca* ceremony. I had truly thought he was nuts, yet here I sat. I know we all fear what we do not understand. I had spoken with many people who had experienced this substance. Please allow me to be very clear right here: this is not about getting high. Nor is it about ingesting something to make you feel good. I also knew there had been those who had gone down and were not prepared at all—not spiritually, mentally, or physically—and it left them mentally deranged. I had even heard stories of those who had wandered off into the jungle and were never seen again. There are areas the locals call places where the *wild peoples* live. They are referring to tribes of a very primitive nature.

CHAPTER 19

My Journey into the Spirit World

THE DAY FINALLY arrived. I first flew to Lima, where the same people from several years earlier met me. Because my flight from the States had arrived later in the day, I had to spend the night in Lima. The next morning, I boarded a small plane to Iquitos. When I landed Eleanor and her local assistant met me. We then got on a boat for a long ride down the Amazon River. When we reached the village, it was so primitive. No electricity and no running water. I was introduced to Don Francisco. Immediately, I connected with him. One look into his eyes and I saw much the same thing I had seen in the Q'ero.

I was to have a private ceremony, but this would happen in a couple of nights. I stayed in this small shack. It was clean and only had a cot to sleep on. There were six other people staying in the camp. Only one spoke English.

A man from England, a professor of something I cannot recall. After we had dinner that evening, we were all sitting outside in a common area. Suddenly it got dark. I mean black dark. I literally could not see my hand in front of me. The canopy of the jungle blocked out all light. This was an experience. Then people sitting in the circle began talking. I know one was German and two were French. Now, I know this may be hard to believe, but we could understand each other. I had taken French in high school but could not speak more than a handful of words and no German. We sat there for a couple of hours talking. This was one of the strangest experiences I have ever had. Finally we were handed flashlights and went to bed.

The next morning, we saw each other at breakfast and could not understand each other, but all of us were amazed this had occurred. That afternoon, Don Francisco came and got me. He took me on a long walk through the jungle. It must have been at least two miles. Finally we arrived at a clearing. There was a creek with a tiny pond, surrounded with this odd color of red mud. I was directed to undress completely and cover my body, head to foot, with the mud. I was to leave one spot on my body clear, so the skin could breathe. I was then directed to sit on the edge of the creek and allow the sun to dry the mud until it was hard. He left me there and said he would return in two hours. Thank God it was a beautiful day of around eighty degrees. I sat there, totally alone, listening to all the wonderful sounds of the jungle. I heard sounds I had never heard and have not heard since. When he did return, I had just gotten back in the water.

Removing this mud was not going to be an easy task. To my amazement, the mud washed off easily. He had brought soap and a clean towel. When I was clean, I cannot begin to describe how I felt. I know there are spas that offer mud baths, but no one had ever described feeling what I felt. I think it may have been the kind of mud I used. Whatever it was, I felt so pure. Don Francisco told me the mud had extracted all the poisons out of my body. He said this would make the initial effects of the *ayahuasca* easier on me.

Eleanor and her assistant, Michael, had returned to her mission near Iquitos but would return the next afternoon. During this time, I hung out, and he had me drink several glasses of a tea he brewed. Normally I would not ingest anything given to me from someone I did not know. For some reason I completely trusted him. When I awakened on that day, I was not allowed to eat any solid food. He continued to give me tea. I was nervous but not overly so. I had a lot of time to think, especially about my *intent*. I had been searching for truth and answers for many years. I wanted to know if there was really life after death of our bodies. I had known I was on the right spiritual path but felt something was missing in me. That afternoon Eleanor and Michael arrived. They were to serve as my protection and guards. She spoke with me quietly and calmed me down. She had taken several *ayahuasca* journeys but no longer needed it. She could go there on her own. Finally the light began to disappear. It was getting dark. I was taken to an area I had not seen since arriving there. It was a grass hut but with no walls.

Don Francisco asked me to open sacred space by calling in the spirits. It is a shamanic prayer. He had me place my mesa out in the middle of the area. There were several candles around and a few burning lights leading into the jungle. He then drank a cup of *ayahuasca*, poured another, and brought it to me. It looked brown or light-rust colored. I began to drink and quickly finished what he had given me. Frankly it tasted horrible. No one said a word, but we were all in continuous prayer and meditation. After twenty or thirty minutes, I was not feeling anything, so he prepared to pour another cup for me. Before he could get it to me, I suddenly became very nauseous and had abdominal pains. I took off into the jungle alone. Trust me, you do not want to hear the details of what occurred then. I was out there at least thirty minutes but closer to forty-five minutes or even an hour. I was flushed out completely.

When I returned, I felt great. I sat down on the dirt floor and soon began a journey I will never forget. Everything went black, and I felt I was traveling at great speed, but into darkness. Suddenly a white light appeared, a circle, and I saw Maggie. She was so far away, and I became fearful.

This feeling was replaced so fast. Then I met these spirits and began talking with them. One looked vaguely familiar, but I could not place him. He began showing me scenes from his life. I recognized my grandmother's house. I saw my mom as a young woman working in the general store they had. Then I knew who he was. He was my maternal grandfather, whom I had never met. He had died two years before I was born. He told me he had always been with me, helping me and watching over me. I wanted to see my mom and dad, my brother, Kathy, and Marty. The answer I received was no, that this was not the time. He assured me they were all doing great and that I would be with them again in time. He told me I had never been alone, and I had many angels with me watching over me constantly. This was the most special feeling I had ever had.

He took me back to when I was a little boy. I saw myself playing alone and fantasizing. Somehow, even then, I felt someone was with me, and I was talking to them. I was accused of talking to myself. He showed me I was not talking to myself, that he was with me as were others. I literally saw my entire life pass before me, one frame at a time. The speed at which this occurred was incredible, but I had no trouble keeping up. Then at some point, I was alone again and in another space. I was being taught many things. This is very difficult to explain, but I will try. I would think a thought and see the energy of that thought travel to the thing or person I was thinking of and see how they were impacted. I was transported back to the time of my drinking. I saw myself telling lies to cover myself. I could trace each lie and see how it had had a negative impact on me and everyone involved. These lies altered my course in life, always in a negative way.

Then I was shown how my life had been changed so dramatically when I got into recovery and began telling the truth. I had been told all my life about being honest and truthful. My parents and teachers had always impressed this on me a zillion times. When I look back, I think I just became oblivious to hearing it. I had learned in my Silva and in my shamanic training that thought moves energy, and energy changes matter. Now I was seeing it vividly. I was shown over and over how this was the key to happiness. I never doubted the importance of honesty in life, but seeing it in this capacity gave it something more—a lot more. It had nothing directly to do with morals, but from a scientific point of view, it was critical. Even quantum physicists have discovered this to be fact. When any of us tell a lie, it complicates our lives in so many ways. One lie can impact our lives negatively for a month, a year, or many years. It produces worry and fear within us. How many times have we heard, "Just tell the truth; the truth will set you free"? We are all made of energy, and we produce energy with not just every word but with every thought. I had always told myself I had never wanted to hurt anyone. While there was truth in this statement, I knew I had, especially when

I was drinking. However, I now learned that I had hurt people by having bad thoughts about them. What amazed me most was how simple this was. I was shown how a lie creates a *log jam* of energy within us. It blocks us, and when our energy is not flowing fluidly, we have problems. I realized this was why the shamanic techniques had proven so effective. Nothing had ever been clearer to me. This was not my opinion but pure fact. If I wanted true happiness, I had to first be honest with myself. If I could not get honest with myself, I could never be honest with others. Simple? Yes. Easy? No! Getting honest with myself would take a lifetime, and it has.

I am still working on it today. No one among us is perfect. We all know this, but if becoming completely honest is not our goal, a major guideline in our lives, we are sure to fail. True happiness can only come from within. The last thing I was shown had to do with a legal matter I was involved in at home. We had a neighbor who had a major anger issue. He had assaulted my wife and kicked our dogs as she was walking them on the street. I had gone over and found him, and he came after me. I hate to admit this, but I had given him a *butt whipping*. The police came, and after speaking with him, no charges were filed. However, he decided to press charges against me. The case was pending in court. I was concerned because my attorney had said that because I had gone to his home, which was where the physical altercation ensued, I could go to jail for assault. At the end of my journey, I saw the entire matter play out in court. Not only was I found not guilty but saw him stop me on the street and apologize to me, my wife, and even to my dogs. Later when I returned home and went to court, it played out exactly as I had seen it. He did catch me walking one of my dogs on the street and did apologize. It happened exactly as I had seen it on my journey.

I finally began to return and to become aware of where I was. Normally, an *ayahuasca* journey lasted six to seven hours. I had been gone for twelve hours. Eleanor was there to welcome me back. So was Don Francisco and Michael. The first words out of my mouth were, "I cannot believe it! It is so darn simple." I must have said it several times before they could ask what was so simple. I explained what I had seen and been shown. Then Don Francisco asked me about my meeting with my grandfather. I was taken back by this. He had gone with me on this part of my journey and had witnessed me communicating with him and the other spirits around me. Then Eleanor began telling me about what she and Michael had observed while I was gone. She said I was lying flat on my back and my body was cold, very cold. Michael had checked my pulse and knew I was still alive. Then I had begun to talk and was clearly having a conversation. Michael had asked, "Who is he talking to?" Eleanor told him I was talking to the spirits. She had been right.

I was still so amazed at what I had been given. I now knew I was never alone and that there is indeed life after life. I had searched for so long and so hard for answers. The key had been under my nose all along. Before this time I knew that honesty was very important. I suppose someone could say I had learned nothing new. On the surface, that was true but equally untrue. I had also known that I needed to stop drinking, but that knowledge had not gotten me sober. I now understood on a whole other level how honesty and/or dishonesty impacted my life in a very real way. I had heard all my life things like, "Thou shall not lie. God will get you for that one, boy." Yes, it was still a question of doing the right thing, but now I could see there was almost a scientific reason to be truthful.

During my journey, the angels kept calling me a name, which made no sense to me. They had continued this throughout my journey. When I returned I did not mention it initially. I was talking nonstop. I remembered how there was no time there. Everything was communicated telepathically. I was outside the confines of space and time. When I thought about a place, I was instantly there. I felt such love and peace that there are no words to describe it. They sat and listened patiently. Eleanor had been there many times; therefore, she understood. Don Francisco had been with me.

Then I told them about the name the spirits had called me. Both just laughed and repeated the same name before

I could even say it. They said, "Harry, in English, your spiritual name is *Shining Bear*." I did not understand, so they explained: a bear represents a soul that has lived many lives. It is what many call an *old soul*. Shining means my light body is very bright compared with others. It is bright white. I then remembered the aura pictures that Maggie and I had taken. Mine was almost pure white. Now I understood. However, I knew Don Francisco had been with me in the spirit world, which explained how he knew. But how did Eleanor know? When I asked her, she told me she had known this from the first time we met at the full-moon fire ceremony, several years earlier. This explained a lot of it, but I still did not understand what it truly meant. They told me I was a very spiritual person and that this was relatively rare. It is commonly seen with prophets, messengers, a few priests, and master shamans. I told them my ego could not handle this.

I know I am not a prophet, but in the years since that time, I do know that I am a messenger. This is why I am writing this book. I have never regretted taking this journey. It did provide the answers I had been seeking for years. However, in retrospect, what it did was give me confirmation of what I already knew. At least in the deep recesses of my soul. It just did it in a very profound way. The final revelation was that I had not so much earned things in my life but was remembering. God knows everything, and God is within everyone. The answers to every question are already inside us. We only need to ask a question, be quiet, and listen for the answer. The challenge is keeping our heads out of the equation. I only know that every single time I listen to my gut, I am right. When I ignore it and go with my head, I live to regret it. I know this is true, but I confess that it is a battle I am still fighting to this day. I can only report that I have improved.

Chapter 20

Processing My Journey

THE FOLLOWING DAY I began my return trip home. I had to spend another night in Lima, but the good news was that it afforded me the opportunity to begin to process what had occurred. I had called Maggie when I got back to Iquitos. She knew what I was planning to do there and was worried. On my flight back to Lima, I began thinking of all the turmoil I had gone through trying to decide whether I should attend an *ayahuasca* ceremony. I knew then I had no regret. I also knew I had no desire to attend another.

Although I did not know it then, I was never again to return to Peru. I had found what I was searching for. I saw just how simple the rules of life were. I am not saying it is easy. But in my case, I could see how I had created most of the complications in my own life. Even in recovery, I had found success in business and had fallen right back into the world of materialism. I had owned three new BMWs and two new Mercedes, along with big, expensive homes. This is why it is so important to slow down and think before I act. I had done well with my nightly prayer and meditations. I would still get up in the morning, rush around, and take off without saying my morning prayers and asking for God's help and guidance. We all know that breakfast is the most important meal of the day, but even more important is morning prayer. God gives us freedom of choice. Every day is a new beginning, a new chance at living. I came to realize that last night's prayer had little to no effect on the next day. I had the choice every morning of asking for God's help and direction or doing it on my own. Every day I do things my way, I end up paying a price I do not wish to pay. For me, I know it is a *control issue*. When I was drinking, there was continuous chaos in my life. I think I became accustomed to it, and it became normal. When my life is running smoothly, I believe that I may subconsciously decide I need some chaos. When I fail to ask for God's help, I always get the chaos. I know God has a sense of humor. I always feel like an idiot and must laugh at myself.

When I returned home to Maggie, I shared everything with her. I told her the spirits had given me a name of "Shining Bear." I explained what it meant, and she was not surprised. Then I recalled something else they told me. Don Francisco had said they saw my mesa, which was lying in the middle of our circle, glowing the entire time. I know there will be people who will say this was just my imagination. I did not see my mesa glowing, but three people did. Additionally, Don Francisco confirmed much of what occurred during this period, especially with my grandfather and the spirits. To me, it does not matter whether it is all true. It does not alter how I live, the tools and truths I adhere to. What I am certain of is there is life after life and that honesty is the key to happiness and inner peace. When I began writing this book, I had decided not to include this part of my story. Then I realized the importance of it. That it was the truth and must be told. However, my concern was that people would misunderstand, that they would think I was advocating the use of drugs. Please allow me to set the record straight: I am totally opposed to the use of all mood- and mind-altering substances. They completely cut us off from our inner soul.

Over the years I discovered that very few people have ever heard of *ayahuasca*. I know many will see it like taking LSD. It is not. I recently watched a video on Prime about the rock band The Who and the composition of their rock opera *Tommy*. Early in the story, Pete Townsend, the composer, had taken a bad trip on LSD. He was on a flight from the US back to England. He described a terrible experience where he left his body. He floated upward and onto the ceiling of the fuselage. However, the instant he left his body, the acid trip stopped completely. He was looking down on himself, on his body. He became terrified. When he got home, he began thinking of what had happened to him. He thought, "I left my body, so I now know I am not my body." I understood this. The acid was only working on his brain. When his spirit left his body, it also left his brain. This is very different from *ayahuasca*. I left my body, leaving my brain behind, and took the journey with my essence, my soul. After Pete's bad trip, he became very antipsychedelic drugs. Someone gave him a book on the teachings of Meher Baba, the great spiritual guru. From there, he became very spiritual and was inspired to write *Tommy*. Again I have never regretted going to the Amazon and having this experience. I knew I was taking a risk but felt it was a calculated one. I took every precaution to mitigate the risk. More importantly I was ready, prepared physically, mentally, and spiritually. I had spent years preparing, although during those years, I was not specifically preparing for an *ayahuasca* experience. Perhaps the most important fact was my purity of *intent*.

I went back to my normal life. I ran my business, spent time with my wife, went to the gym, and was very happy and content. I also continued teaching the medicine wheel for the Four Winds Group. Most of the classes were held in Utah. As a few years passed, I found I was becoming disillusioned. I loved teaching the classes but began noticing the classes were becoming larger. Many of the *students* clearly had issues and, in my opinion, should not have been there. They needed help, professional help. Before any of us can help others, we must first take care of ourselves, deal with our own issues. I am very aware that the more I know about me, the better I understand others. The prospect of these individuals trying to heal others was frightening. It would have been like having me run a group therapy session my first week in treatment. The blind leading the blind. I have known a few people who got PhDs in psychology thinking they could fix themselves. Sorry, it does not work like that. To be a great healer, especially of the mind, you must first be healed yourself.

When I quit drinking, I carried a load of guilt for at least ten years. Most of my guilt was about my decisions, bad choices following Kathy's death. I was in bondage. As I dealt with all my issues, all my demons, I slowly came to accept myself and every mistake I had made. The more I accepted myself, the more I accepted others. I might not agree with people or approve of what they were doing, but I understood them. I could see where they were on their journey. Anyway I became more and more concerned about what I was witnessing with people coming onto the path. The bottom line is that it was about money. I also felt I had received all I was going to internally.

Alberto was not around very often, and I did not think he knew what was going on. I ended up meeting him in Sedona, where I assisted him with a two-day seminar. I then drove him back to the airport in Phoenix. I explained what I had observed, and he agreed with me. I also told him I felt I was at the end of the path. He was not surprised. He asked if I wanted to go to another level, a deeper one. He told me about a man living in the mountains, near Tahoe. I did fly there and meet with this man. He may have been the most powerful shaman I have ever met. In the end, I decided not to move forward. To go deeper could destroy the world and life I had. Besides it was now time to use everything I had learned. Thank God I did not go that direction. I had no idea what was to come into my life.

Chapter 21

Another Trauma

In March of 2009, I had to have total reconstructive surgery on my right foot. I was working out in a gym in Scottsdale on a seated calf press. I had a lot of weight on it when my left toe slipped off. All the weight then concentrated in the arch of my right foot. I had always had very high arches, and gradually the entire arch collapsed. It did not look like the foot of a human anymore. Following the surgery, I was told I could not place any weight on the foot for eight weeks, not even to balance myself. For a man that had been highly active, constantly on the move, this was not a good experience. The worst parts were the post-op infections. I had many PICC lines for IV antibiotics.

In that year, I had four surgeries. I was unable to work, and the San Francisco–based company Maggie had been with filed for bankruptcy. So we were both unemployed. As a private business owner, I had private insurance. My premiums were increased to $1,600 per month, just for me.

With some medical expenses, they paid 80 percent, some 50 percent, and some nothing. We were not out of pocket thousands of dollars, not even tens of thousands, but hundreds of thousands of dollars. In the end it wiped us out. By early 2012, I was walking again. We decided to move back to Atlanta. We had never felt at home in Arizona, and most of our family were on the East Coast. My business had never thrived there as it had in Atlanta. I needed to earn money fast. Perhaps the worst part for me spiritually was that I had been compelled to take many pain killers. They are never good for anyone in recovery, but I was aware they were blocking me from my inner self, from my soul. When we returned to Atlanta, Maggie signed a contract for a new position the day we moved into the home we had rented. My business took off immediately. A few months passed, and another issue with my foot appeared. I ended up having three more surgeries. At least we were working, but it was very difficult for me. To sit at a desk on a computer and on the phone with my foot on the floor created havoc. The foot would swell, and the pain became intolerable. By the end of 2014, my foot was finally healed. I do not know which of us had the worst end of this, me or Maggie. It has never been easy for me to ask for help, but during this time, she had to wait on me like a baby. Watching her doing her chores and mine tore me to pieces inside. She never complained. She just accepted it, like we had been taught. It certainly did instill a lot of humility inside me. We have finally bought a new home, have two Honda Accords, and adopted a simple life, which we both love. This had been a real tragedy and would have destroyed most marriages. Instead it brought us closer than ever. We went through every step together.

For five years things went well. Then I began feeling bad all the time. It felt like the flu. I did have some respiratory infections, but none of it made any sense to me. I was feeling worse and worse all the time. Then we found the truth. One Sunday evening I sat on the side of the bed to remove my shoes and socks. When I looked down, I saw something dark on my white athletic socks. On my right foot. The sock was full of blood. The bottom of my foot was covered with blood blisters. This had all appeared in less than twelve hours. We were both stunned. By 11:00 a.m. the following day, we were sitting in front of my orthopedist. He gave us two options. He said he could do more surgery or amputate. We said nothing at the time but later learned we were thinking the same thing. We had both had enough. We made the decision for amputation when we returned to our car. I realize this may sound strange, but I was relieved. I had been concerned over my health. My doctors could not give me any answers. There was no external evidence that there was anything going on with my foot. All our family and friends thought this had to be a difficult decision for us, but it was not. No one other than my sister had any idea of what we had been through.

My sister, Carolyn, knew because she had come down to take care of me for a few days when Maggie had to go out of town for business. Before she left she told us that, although she thought she understood what we had endured, she had no idea until she saw it and lived it with me. It was nearly impossible to explain to anyone, including our family and best friends. It was bad enough that I was unable to walk for long periods, but to be flat on my back with infections, sick and nauseous, was devasting. It tested our faith to the maximum. We got through it because our faith never cracked. I suppose we are all good Monday morning quarterbacks, but I had said many times that had I known what was to come back in 2009 when I had the first surgery, I would have chosen amputation then.

I had the surgery on a Tuesday afternoon. I was completely ready. I knew I was not alone. I had done a lot of prayer and meditation, and I could feel the presence of the Lord and my angels around me constantly. I do not say this lightly. I literally could feel it. When I awakened the next morning in a hospital room, I felt like a million dollars, like my old self. I realized that by removing the foot, they had also removed the poison from the infection. I immediately began screaming to go home. Then two people from the prosthetic company arrived to take some measurements. They had seen many people the morning after amputations, as had my nurses. They said they had never seen anyone look that good. They are still talking about it. I was discharged and back home hours after my surgery. I later learned that most amputees remain in the hospital for at least a few days. I know one man who spent two weeks there.

Maggie was once again having to take care of me like a baby. She never once complained, and neither did I. I had God and my angels with me every minute. I maintained a positive attitude, and not once did I feel self-pity or regret on the decision. People often say that we discover who our true friends are when the chips are down. I certainly did. I had many family members and friends calling me constantly. My sponsor, Bob, my best friend, David, and my close friend, Carlisle, called me every single day. Sometimes it would be for just a minute, but they wanted me to know they were there for me. Many others called three to four times every week and texted me. The time passed quickly.

We lived for the day I would receive my new leg, my prosthesis. Before my surgery a close friend had introduced me to a man who had had the same surgery, on the same right leg, six months earlier. He proved to be the epitome of a positive attitude. He threw an amputation party before his surgery and another when he received his prosthesis. I loved this man and still do. We had chosen a company with state-of-the-art technology. They build your prosthesis in one day.

When the day arrived, we got there at 9:00 a.m. We left at 3:30 p.m. with my new foot and lower leg. This was a

Wednesday. The next day a physical therapist came to our home and helped me get it on and take a few steps. It was painful, but he had a rope around my waist for protection. The next day I was to repeat what he had done with me. I realized that this would require weeks before I could get around. My friend Mike had shared with me how he did it by walking around the kitchen, holding onto the counters. So I had Maggie roll me into the kitchen, with my prosthesis on. I got up and began walking around the kitchen, holding onto the counters. It was easy for me. I was unable to make a full circle because there was a pantry door and refrigerator and no counters. I decided to just walk across and did with ease. Once I realized I could do that, I began walking all over the downstairs. Maggie watched in amazement. Then I walked upstairs, but only one step at a time. I walked around up there. I was now thinking this is easy. I was planning on driving the next day. But when I got up the next morning, my leg was so sore and swollen, I could not even get my prosthesis on. I had overdone it.

I called my people at the prosthetic company and told them what had occurred and received a ration of criticism. They told me to only work with the PT guy. By Monday, my leg was fine, and I was back in business. I cancelled the PT guy two days later. I was concerned about being able to drive, but Mike had told me it was nothing to worry about. He was right. I had to go for a follow-up appointment exactly two weeks after receiving my prosthesis. When they saw me drive into the parking lot alone, walk inside with not even a cane, they appeared to be in shock. I was told that no one drives themselves, and most arrive for their follow-up on a walker. Why was it so different for me? I used prayer and meditation. I visualized Mike walking around his kitchen and then visualized myself walking around mine. I used mind control I had learned years earlier. I not only had no self-pity but was full of gratitude. I had an enormous amount of moral support. Most important was that I had the Lord and my angels with me every step of the way.

Maggie and I were delighted. I am not saying this was an easy time for us, but life often deals challenges, to quote the phrase, "We must play the cards we are dealt." I understand when I talk about having God and angels with me, most people think, "Yeah, yeah, I have heard that one before." When I say it, I do not mean it figuratively but literally. Because of the journey my life has taken me on, this is not my opinion, but what I know. I have experienced this so many times that I finally gave up second-guessing myself.

Years earlier I had experienced God's presence in my life and had said to myself, "It is just my imagination, all in my head." Then I would immediately be shown again and again that it was not my imagination. Eventually I would become embarrassed at myself for even going there. We literally do create our own reality. We have choices every day. God also knows I have made many poor choices. The difference today, as opposed to my early life, is that I accept full responsibility for every one of them. It is not and has never been a question of whether we make mistakes. The determining factor is what we choose to do afterward. This is what determines the quality of our life, inner peace, and happiness.

Chapter 22

Realizations

MANY YEARS AGO, I watched a John Wayne movie called *Angel and the Badman*. He played the badman. He encountered a family of Quakers after being shot. They took care of him, and he fell in love with the daughter, the angel. There were several families of Quaker farmers living in a valley. Then a man purchased the land on the mountain above them, where the water originated from. This man dammed up the stream and cut off their water. When John Wayne's character was told of this, he asked what they had done. He guessed they prayed for water. The mother said, "No, we prayed for the man." Wayne said, "Let me get this straight. He turned off your water, and you prayed for him?" She said, "Of course. Can you not see? By committing an evil act, the poor man injured his soul."

At the time I thought this funny and that these people were nuts. Now I get it. If you visualize your soul as a light body, white, as an energy field around you, then you can understand where we all begin at birth. Deep down, we all know right from wrong, every single one of us—the only possible exception is those with a serious mental illness. As we age we may be taught many wrongs. As teenagers we choose a group of friends who are all engaged in one form of evil or another. Perhaps they are doing drugs, committing criminal acts, etc. We may begin to feel we are doing nothing wrong because it seems everyone else is doing the same thing. Of course these behaviors are still very wrong but have just been normalized because of the group of people we spend our time with. Thus the life advice of "always stick with the winners." Every single time we do anything we know within to be wrong, we place a black mark on our spirit body. As we continue doing these wrongs, eventually our spirit body becomes totally black. Then we are living in darkness, cut off from God, from the universe, from love, and from our inner self. This may sound like a crazy analogy to you, but I know this to be accurate. I have seen it with myself years ago and on many people since. We also know there is a little good in the worst of us and a little bad in the best of us. Both good and evil exist in all living things. There are two people inside you; there is the person you want to be and the person you do not want to be. We all have both, and we all have a choice. Fight the person you do not want to be and feed the person you want to be. We all make mistakes and bad choices and do bad things at some stage of our lives. God knows I have made my share and then some.

My light had gone out in the mideighties. I was dead for all intents and purposes. Today the spirits call me Shining Bear. To get from death to life required an enormous amount of help and work. I began removing the black marks from my spirit body one at a time. I did this by getting honest with myself and others. I admitted every wrong to myself, to God, and to another human being. Then I started making amends and setting things right. I still recall many friends and family members telling me how proud they were of me for stopping drinking. I was embarrassed by this every time because I cannot take any credit for my sobriety. If I could have done it myself, there would have been no need for me to enter any of the treatment centers. God removed the obsession and compulsion to drink. To doubt this would be insanity. If you ask anyone in long-term recovery who got them sober, they will give you the same answer. My sobriety is literally a miracle. I really hate to say this, but so many never stay clean and sober. They either die or end up in jail or an insane asylum. I have witnessed so much of this, including people I went through treatment with. Some I lived with.

I have known so many who claim to be atheist. They live inside their heads and can convince themselves that God does not exist. I have never personally known an atheist who was happy or who was not full of anger. Perhaps there are some, but I have never seen one. There is the old saying, "There are no atheists in foxholes." I grew up during the Vietnam War. I had several close friends that ended up in combat. They shared stories of friends they had gone through bootcamp with who had claimed to be atheist. When the bullets began whizzing by their heads, and they saw close friends blown to pieces, they heard, "God, please help me." Likewise we have seen many enter AA and claim to be atheist. Any reference to God and they become angry. This is exactly why the founders of AA chose to use the expression "higher power" instead of God. Normally when we see a person begin to "get it" and stay sober for a while, suddenly they begin changing to God as their higher power.

I have arrived at an understanding that God is our creator. God is within every human heart, in every living thing. To deny this is the height of arrogance. However, the minute someone mentions God, people immediately think of religion. I do not! To me religion is man-made and, therefore, full of flaws and misinterpretations. Make no mistake, I love Jesus Christ with all my heart and soul. He is with me this minute and directed me every step in writing this book. Technically I am a Christian. I believe in all the teachings of Christ. He taught love, not fear. He did not dwell on going to church. He told us to love each other. He taught nonjudgment, peace on earth. He also taught us there is an afterlife, that we do not die, just our bodies. There is great power in many people praying collectively. However, for me, it is all about my personal relationship with Jesus. I used to pray to God but could not visualize God. I can visualize Jesus; therefore, it became more personal to me.

Most Christians believe that if you are not a Christian you go to hell. This is because they say the only way to God is through Jesus Christ. To me, the only was is through the practice of the teachings of Christ. Many spiritual gurus have taught the same things before and after Jesus walked on this earth. To me, it is what is in our hearts. When I met the Q'ero, I would have given anything for what I saw in their eyes. Yet they had never heard of Jesus. There is no way I am going to believe that God would have them burn in hell for eternity. You or I might be able to fool other people but not God. He knows what is in our hearts. To me, the Ten Commandants are not religious but universal truths. You will find them in the teachings of every spiritual teacher from Gandhi, to Jesus, to Mohammad, to Buddha, etc. We have all known individuals who attend church every Sunday and yet know them to be crooks. Again it is what is in your heart. You either live the teachings in every corner of your life, or you do not.

When we make a mistake or commit an act we know to be wrong, we have a choice. We can own it and assume full responsibility or not. Many seem to think that by admitting their wrongdoing, people will think less of them. In my experience, this is not true. I believe people are starved to death for truth and honesty. Regardless of what they might say at the time, they will respect you for your honesty. "The truth will set you free" is a statement we have all heard many times. Living it is the key. Being honest with others is important, but we must first be honest with ourselves. This is so simple but not easy. It takes a lifetime. If we fail to adopt this as a guideline in our lives, working on it every single day, we are doomed to a miserable existence.

Jesus and other spiritual gurus have taught us to love each other. I have always had a lot of love inside me. I loved my family, my wife, my animals, and my closest friends. When my drinking got bad, I hated everyone. I can now see that it was because I hated myself. When I got into recovery and began clearing my mind and soul, I got back to my old loving self. However, it took years of working on me before I could even come close to loving my fellow humans. I was carrying too much guilt from my drinking days to fully love myself. I finally realized I would never be perfect. I had to reach a point of acceptance of myself and who I am, flaws and assets alike. When I got there, I could begin accepting others I encountered.

Music has always influenced me. The reason is that many writers of musical lyrics are coming from their heart. Years ago Paul McCartney wrote a song with the following words: "You would think the world has had enough silly love songs, but I look around me and know it isn't so, oh no." He is right. We never get enough love. We all want to be loved and to love. However we allow ourselves to get so unbalanced between darkness and light within, we can neither give nor receive love. Some years ago, it was suggested to me that whenever I meet anyone, I silently say, "I love you." I tried it for a few weeks. Initially I did not notice much difference. Then suddenly I was shocked to see the difference in how people responded to me. This included people who were angry. I later realized the reason I did not notice a significant difference at first was because by saying "I love you," I was being changed. I still use this technique today.

We really are all connected, brothers and sisters. Life's energy passes through me to you and from you to your family and friends. A major discovery I made when in early recovery had to do with *uniqueness*. I was so full of shame, self-loathing, and a wide cross section of feelings, that I felt unique. I had trouble sharing any of my feelings because I could not imagine anyone else had ever felt what I had. When they finally squeezed them out of me, I was shocked to hear others laugh at me. Not at me but with me. Many of these people laughing had been around much longer than me. Every single one of them had felt the same things as I had. Then the joke became, "Wow, you are *unique*." We are not that different. Feelings are feelings in every human being.

I met and spent a lot of time with people from Europe, South America, and Asia. As we talked and shared, I realized they were just like me, every one of them. It does not matter whether we are rich or poor, educated or not, or what color our skin is; we are all human. In AA, we say alcoholism is the great leveler. We get all walks of life, just like any other disease. I have seen truck drivers sponsoring doctors. We choose a sponsor based upon that person having within what we want. What we want in terms of quality of sobriety, spirituality, and what we see inside that person.

The Golden Rule is do unto others as you wish done unto you. This is not religious but has been around throughout mankind's history. It is just common sense to me. To have a successful culture, this rule must be applied. Confucius said this many years before Jesus appeared. I often ask myself "*Why* is this so hard for people to apply?" How have we become so selfish? *Why* is it so difficult for us to see that the better we all do in life, the better we as individuals do? We have all known people who gossip continually, putting others down. This used to upset me, but now I truly feel sorry for such people. They are always the ones most unhappy, with the most issues in their lives. They think that by putting someone down they are somehow elevated. The opposite is true. If you want to elevate yourself, then help others to rise above what may be going on in their lives.

Recently I was listening to an old Pink Floyd song called "Echoes," within the lyrics, "Strangers passing in the street. By chance two separate glances meet, and I am you and what I see is me." I had heard this song decades ago but never heard the words. I was really struck by the power and truth in these lyrics. Roger Waters wrote this and was a young man, probably in his early twenties.

Some of us are far more sensitive than others. It is rare, in my experience, to find this kind of depth in a young adult. Most of us are too busy having fun and trying to get stuff for ourselves. Most of us begin to awaken around thirty-five to forty-five years of age. By then we have gotten most everything that was supposed to make us happy. Then one day we begin asking ourselves, "Is this all there is?" Then we begin to awaken spiritually. We may start going to church, hoping something will stick or that we will hear something that will provide us with the key. Sadly what most never do is look within their own heart and begin to clean house. Get honest with themselves, hold themselves fully accountable for anything and everything wrong within their lives. In short they fail to take any action of the nature of what I have written within this book.

I know there will be those who may say, "Yes, but much of what Harry talks about is for alcoholics." Please allow me to be clear: the twelve steps have nothing to do with alcohol. There is nothing original in the program, other than the fact it was reorganized into a twelve-step format that is easy to follow. The steps are designed to produce a spiritual awakening within the individual. They can and have produced spiritual awakenings in many people, not just alcoholics. We know that most people believe in some form of higher power but never pray, much less meditate. I believe the reason for this is because of a guilty conscious. We intuitively know we cannot trick God. We simply cannot drop to our knees and pray with a guilty conscious, but this is what we must do. If I really feel bad about something I have done, it takes more than just saying I am sorry to make it right. Still this is where we begin. We admit our wrong to ourselves, to God, and wherever possible, to the person(s) we have wronged and become willing to make it right. I recall the first time I did this. It felt like a ton of weight had been lifted from me. I so loved the way it made me feel that I was hungry for more. I know there will be people who will think this is all much ado about nothing. Believe me, I understand because I thought the same way. This is why I went through four twenty-eight-day treatments, followed by a long-term recovery program in MARR. I was *dead* by the time I reached the fourth program, the psychiatric hospital. Many members of my family could never accept that I was an alcoholic. They said, "Harry had a nervous breakdown from all the deaths."

Another important point I need to make is this: even after I had been sober for several years, I thought my life had been wonderful before Kathy was diagnosed and my parents died. It was not a bad life. I know how much I loved Kathy and my parents. In retrospect, on the outside it was a normal and successful life. Today looking back, I know I was an alcoholic from the beginning, but worse, I was asleep. In spiritual language, I was deaf, blind, and dumb. I was completely unaware of the spiritual world around me. Unlike today I could not stand on a mountain looking at trees and see the energy emanating from them and all living things. I do not like saying it, but I was just like 90 percent of other people. Once I stopped drinking, I had many people tell me how proud they were of me. I have said this many times before, but I honestly cannot take any credit for my sobriety. God lifted it from me, period. Even then I was not awake. I had just come to. Once I had had a taste of the happiness I sought, I wanted more and more. I practiced the principles in all my affairs; I did everything suggested of me. Once the use of the tools became a part of me, I began reading and studying. I wanted happiness through spiritual enlightenment. I went after it with a vengeance. In the end, I found what I had been looking for. I found the answers to my questions. I had come from death to life.

Chapter 23

Conclusion

In conclusion, I leave a message, especially to my family and to young people. Ask yourself the question I was asked many years ago: What do you want out of life? If you are honest with yourself, the answer will be *happiness*. To survive in our society, you will need money. To get a good job, you will need education and training. Then you need shelter, food, clothing, transportation, insurance, and enough to take a decent vacation occasionally. You also need enough left over to save for a rainy day. Beyond this, you do not *need* more. Please believe me, I found this out the hard way. Maggie and I lived in huge homes and drove very expensive cars for years. We found these things never made us happy. On the contrary, they complicated our lives and became anchors around our necks.

What money can do for you, if you save it, is give you freedom. Freedom to choose freely. I have seen many people stay in jobs they despise and work for people they cannot respect because they have no viable options. They have families to feed. If you really want to be happy, you must look within your own heart. You must take full responsibility for yourself. We often say, "Life is a journey." This is true, but like with any journey, we need a road map. There is no GPS in your own heart. It is, therefore, critical that you adopt the tools and spiritual principles put forth here. I did not create one. They have been around for millennia. There are no personal opinions, no politics here. These are universal truths that can never be changed. We either adhere to them or suffer the consequences, as many of us have. To me, it does not matter what church you select, if any at all. This is your choice. Just never follow a man. Follow God and your own heart. If you follow your head only, God help you because no one else can. Your only true responsibility is to always do the best you can. Leave the results up to God. Spending your life worrying about the results or trying to force the results is a waste of life. Watch out what you pray for because you might just get it. Accept the fact that none of us can see how a given result may affect our life down the road. Accept life as it is and always practice gratitude.

When I watch the news, I see so many things I disagree with, things that once would have upset me, but in the end, I know I must accept what it is for now. If there is nothing I can do about it, then why spend my time worrying about it. If you are a parent and want your kids to have a good life, perhaps better than you had, teach them all these principles. Give them these tools.

What really confuses me the most is this: these truths have been around throughout history, yet most people ignore them. Many have never heard of them. We have 24-7 media coverage today. The talking heads bantering on and on about the problems we face but never mentioning these truths. It is not politically correct to mention God. Can you imagine how our society would change if everyone suddenly began practicing these principles and using these tools? I recognize this is not going to occur overnight. Evil will always be present. It must start by teaching our children. I hear so many people say, "We give our kids everything, things we never had growing up." What they mean is they are giving them everything money can buy. Many fail to give them the most important things in life, which are these tools to live by. We now know that a child's basic values and morals are established by age eight. Some say earlier than that. The best way to teach is by example. Telling a kid to do as I say, not as I do, simply does not work.

One of the saddest statistics today is the divorce rate. Many times, this destroys the lives of the couple involved. However, when there are children involved, the divorce is devasting for them. Every adult has witnessed the negative impact this has on children. This is not only what it does to them at the time but for years to come. Many of them grow up, get married, and they, too, become a statistic of divorce. Many of these divorced couples end up marrying again and again, with the same result. The main reason for this is they carry the same baggage from one marriage into another.

I have been blessed with two incredible marriages. Maggie and I have been asked many times, "What is the secret?" There is no secret, unless you consider complete honesty to be one. It takes two mentally and spiritually healthy people to have a great marriage. Maggie and I were both relatively happy before our first date. Neither of us needed anyone else, nor were we searching for someone else to make us happy. Both of us had some baggage, but the critical thing was that we shared everything with each other. We have never had secrets between us. Here again I have seen couples meet and fall in love. They fail to be honest with each other because of *fear* of losing the other. I assure you that, if the love is real, most people will accept your past mistakes, especially if you own them and have learned from them. It doesn't matter how big or how small the mistakes were. However, if you fail to disclose the truth prior to the marriage, and the person discovers the truth much later, even the small mistakes you concealed can destroy the marriage. It is not just about the mistake itself, but it can destroy *trust*. When there is an absence of trust in a marriage, you have nothing. Besides you might as well tell it all anyway because I assure you that, in time, the truth will always surface. The world is indeed full of trickery, but if you possess that spiritual bond between you and your spouse at home, it will give you a safe refuge. It will provide the balance within that we all need.

When I have a conflict going on in my life, Maggie always knows. After decades of marriage, she rarely says a word about it. She just allows me to suffer with it for a couple of days. She knows I will come to her with the truth. I always do, but so does she. I am just a bit slower than her, but the truth always prevails. I can report this truth: a good marriage is one of the greatest gifts in life. It is certainly true for Maggie and me. I have seen so many marriages fail, and the children pay the price. Yes, complete honesty from both parties is a must. But perhaps equally critical is that the two people involved must come to the table happy to begin with.

Here again we all seek happiness, and this is a valid intention. The problem is that we look to find it outside ourselves—this can be a new car, a new home, a new job, or even a different location. Enduring happiness is only found by going within our own heart. Everything else—though these things can bring the quick fix of happiness—is only temporary. The new always wears off, and we find ourselves back with the same misery we had before. Only by going within and using the tools I have described within the pages of this book will you discover true and lasting happiness and joy in your life.

Lastly we always attract that which we are. When you connect with another happy person, fall in love, and marry, you will find this person can augment your happiness in incredible ways. This is especially true when both parties are growing along the same spiritual lines.

Always follow your own heart. Listen to the little voice from within. This is God within and exists in every human heart. Use your head but only as a tool. That is all it is. Learn to be still, be quiet, and listen. Pray every day of your life but then listen. It has been said that bad things happen to good people. I know this is true, but if you follow the spiritual truths, these bad things can mold you, teach you, and become the best things that ever happen to you. I am living proof of this fact. It has also been said that it is easy to be a great man/woman when you are on top of the mountain. What determines the true quality of the person is how they handle it when deep within the valley. Learn to see the so-called bad things that occur in your life as *opportunities for growth*. Nothing lasts forever, so always remember, when you are in these valleys, the famous words, "This, too, shall pass away."

I have endured many losses and terrible hardships in my life. I came to the life I now have from the depths of hell. Today when I consider from where I came, because of the path I chose, I can only think of the cliché, "You cannot get here from there." I have had experiences on my life journey that few others have had. I have had many people tell me I am a very wise person. I am just me. Wise compared with whom? I can only say that whatever wisdom I have has come from the worst times of my life and not the best. This has all led me to a *knowing*, not a belief. In the final analysis, *love* is the only thing that matters, and God is pure love. I know that I have discovered a humility through the realization that I am just a white speck on the wall of the universe. I also know my tiny speck shines a bright white, thus my spiritual name, Shining Bear. I am no more special to God than you are. I love my life but neither am I afraid of the death of my body. I sure look forward to meeting the Lord. I am not in a rush to do so, but at my age, I know it will not be long.

We will always have freedom of choice. We can choose love, or we can choose fear. Every single day is a new beginning, and we must choose every morning. I am surrounded by love, but I also know how easy it is to slip into fear. Evil does exist in the world and the universe. To think otherwise would be the height of naivety. Almost every time I turn on the news, evil is staring me in the face. We all must make the choice. I choose love. It is the only path to happiness, which has always been my goal in life.

What I have written is not my opinion. The tools and principles contained here are time tested and proven—not only by myself but also by millions of people throughout human history. Every successful civilization in history has adhered to them. Many of these civilizations failed later as a direct result of moral decay and failure of its people to practice the principles that had once brought them happiness and success. These truths have been taught by every spiritual teacher in our written history. They have been lost and rediscovered many times. Truth is truth, and you may try to deny it, but in the end it will always surface, again and again.

I have had a few people look around and say, "What difference can I make?" The country is falling apart. I answer by saying this: Just because many other people choose to be miserable, why should you? We all have the same choices. In addition, by being a person of light, a person of God, you can impact every single human you encounter. People always respond well to love and happiness and will begin to wonder what you have. They will want it for themselves. A single person of God can indeed impact the world around them. This has happened countless times throughout history. We are only here for such a short time. The only thing we leave with is love. The real question is, "What do you leave with, if you fail to find love?" We leave with nothing, and this is for an eternity.

My true prayer is that you will choose wisely. I ask you to love me, love yourself, and love each other. I wish all of you Godspeed!

Epilogue

Earlier in this story, I disclosed that I had been given a book called *Life after Life*, by Dr. Raymond Moody. This occurred shortly after Kathy had died. Although I was intoxicated during that time, it had a huge impact on me. It had a ring of truth to me, and I never forgot it. The book was written from the perspective of Dr. Moody, a medical doctor. I read this book nearly forty years ago. Although I was not aware, there has since been massive amounts of research in this area. Back then most of the *death-and-backers*, as they are often called, kept their experiences private due to the stigma attached to the topic. When some tried telling what had happened, people thought them crazy, and they were even placed in psychiatric hospitals. Today the topic is so pervasive that more and more people have come forward to describe their near-death experiences.

Today there are tens of thousands of documented cases from all over the world. Today we can hear from the perspectives of the near-death experiencers (NDEs) themselves. Although there are differences in the stories, most have had identical things occur. Perhaps the most common occurrence was the profound impact it had on everyone when they returned. Some had been atheist or agnostic, and others did believe in God prior to the event. When they returned, not a single one I read about had any doubt there is a God, a heaven, and a hell. I recently watched a documentary about four individuals, three women and one man. None wanted to return because all felt more alive there than ever before. They met with God and Jesus and were taught many lessons. The key lesson was that *love* is all that mattered. There was no judgment at all. Each were shown a life review, from birth to their death. All had sinned, but when these things were shown, they still felt no judgment but sadness. God still loved them so much. A great deal of what they were shown had to do with how they had treated others in life. They saw how one little act of kindness could make a tremendous impact.

Conversely they saw how one small act of anger could produce so much harm. While teaching a young mother, God held a stone in his hand and said, "The stone is you, the light within you is me, and I am always with you." God then dropped the stone, and together they watched it fall into a huge body of water without shores. God told her the water was humankind. When the rock struck the water, there was a huge splash. Then they observed the ripples as they multiplied and expanded. He said, "Every word you speak, every thought you have, and every action you take represents one of these ripples." The truth of the lesson was to demonstrate the universal laws of cause and effect. Once we think a negative thought or commit a negative action, the energy is set into motion, and there is no stopping it. There will be an effect.

Early in the research, most doctors did not believe any of this was real. However, there were many patients who had died on operating room tables. These experiences always begin with the soul being released from the body. Many would then hover there for a while, hearing every word that was spoken and seeing every action taken. When these patients were resuscitated, they described to the surgeons everything they had seen and heard. The surgeons would think this impossible, but there it was with no other possible explanation. This has led to many members of the medical community waking up to this phenomenon. In response, this has led to massive amounts of research. Patients are no longer considered crazy, which has resulted in more and more of these people revealing their experiences.

There are so many commonalities among the NDEs, such as they all report going into a tunnel and seeing a bright light at the end. There, many are greeted by deceased family members and friends who have gone before them. While there, time has no meaning nor does distance. There is no pain, no suffering—only pure love and on a scale that none can begin to describe. When they were told they must return, no one wanted to. Their lives were changed forever. Their priorities in this life were completely reversed. Other than what they needed to survive, money and material possessions no longer had meaning for them. They devoted their lives to God, to love, and to helping others.

It has been close to twenty years since I took the *ayahuasca* journey in the jungle. In recent years, I have occasionally caught myself drifting back into my head, into my intellect. I have often said when I am in my head, I am in enemy territory. Although I usually mean it as a joke, like all jokes, there is an element of truth. In my case, this created some doubt within me. I even caught myself questioning God and everything I had learned. When I began reading more about these cases of near-death experiences and from the perspective of those who have had them, it brought what I had discovered over many years full circle. For years, I told people I had discovered the *key to happiness*, which is self-honesty. Lies are almost always based in fear. Fear and love cannot coexist in the same moment. Through my training in mind control, I had experienced the power of *cause and effect*, that thought moves energy, and energy changes matter. I had learned and experienced how critical the practice of nonjudgment is. Above all else, I know that in the final analysis of life, *love* is all that matters. I had discovered that in any given moment we are either coming from within ourselves from a place of love, or fear. To come from love, we must have a clean conscience. To have a clean conscience, we must be honest with ourselves and with others. We must be at peace within our own heart. So why do we lie? For many of us, this begins when we are kids. We break rules and lie to cover it up. We are afraid of the consequences. As adolescents, we desire acceptance from our peers. Fear of not being accepted for who we really are often brings dishonesty. These same patterns follow us into adulthood.

I always felt inferior growing up. I lied while attempting to make myself appear to be more than what I was. Much of that seems silly to me today, but it launched a pattern of behavior and lying that became a terrible habit. When I began to face my character flaws and correct them, I began feeling peaceful inside my own skin. As humans, none of us is perfect. God gave all of us *freedom of choice*. He will never take this away from us. There exist good and evil in every human soul. We must choose every single minute of every day. Once we tell a lie, then that lie must become true. So this launches a domino effect of one lie following another. "Oh, what a tangled web we weave." This creates conflict in the soul, and there can be no inner peace. If we want love, if we want happiness, if we want peace, we must get honest with ourselves and eliminate this inner conflict. How can we be honest with anyone else if we are not first honest with ourselves. We have all heard it said, "The truth will set you free." ow can we be honestH

The death-and-backers learned all of this within minutes on one day. It has taken me a lifetime, searching for truth and happiness, to arrive to the exact same conclusions. Life truly is so darn simple, but complicated. Why is it complicated? I know it is about our gift of freedom of choice. We think we know what is best for us and listen to our head, not our heart. God knows that I am far from a perfect person, but I also know he loves me and is proud of the man I have become. Left to my own devices, I would not have entered the business I was perfect for. God has blessed us for decades. I would have never found my marriage to Maggie, which is truly a marriage made in heaven.

The recent documentary on NDEs, involving four individuals, did bring me to a new realization that I had found truth in my life. One of the four was only three years old when she drowned in a tank of water. The experience completely changed the path of her life. I could not help wondering how my life would have been different had I known then what I know today. What a gift she was given. We all must play the cards we are dealt in life. I now realize I was not awake to the world around me in the early years of my life. I had to endure many hardships and losses before I was ready and spiritually prepared to have God enter my life. What a journey I have had. I am not alone and have never been, even within my darkest hours.

I end this story by saying this: God allowed me the freedom of choice in my early life, but although he was always with me, I ran on self-will alone. God was watching me the entire time. I am certain he was sad to observe my choices but did not intervene until I asked. The moment I found myself hopeless and got on my knees and asked for help from the bottom of my heart, he then came to my rescue. I point out that my prayer was not a foxhole one, but from deep within me. From that moment forward and to this day, he has always been with me. He guides me in my every thought, word, and deed. I know some people will not believe this. Well, I am human and have questioned it myself; however, God has proven it to me so many times over the years. When I recall all these times, there is simply no way a sane person could have doubt.

Even with everything I have lived through and encountered in my life, there is still a piece of me that wants proof. I know I am far from being alone in this manner of thinking. Like most educated people, I look for data, a lot of hard facts, to arrive at a conclusion. If you are reading this and truly want to know truth, then look at the tens of thousands of cases of documented near-death experiences. Most of the clinical data comes from medical doctors. These people are scientists and were taught this is not possible in medical schools. However, the amount of hard data is so overwhelming they simply cannot deny the truth. While it is true there are still many in the medical community who still do not accept this as fact, most simply have not been exposed to it within their own practices.

I am not asking you to take my word for it, but before you dismiss it as crazy, do your own due diligence. Just keep an open mind. This means not to bring your own preconceived notions into it. A scientist can never be scientific if he/she comes into an investigation with prejudices.

The truth you will find can alter your life in a very profound and positive way. Yes, it took me decades to discover these same truths. When we have personal experiences and the results are repeated over and over again, we arrive at a deep knowing that cannot easily be taken away. Yet when I found all the data on NDEs, it certainly gave me not only confirmation but also validation. I sincerely pray that you will not only come to believe but also incorporate the daily practice of these truths into your life. Do this, and I promise you will find a new happiness and joy in your life that you never thought possible.

www.ingramcontent.com/pod-product-compliance
Lightning Source LLC
Chambersburg PA
CBHW032105090426
42743CB00007B/248